COMPILED ORDINANCES

OF THE

CITY OF EAST SAGINAW,

TITLE I.

OF THE CITY OFFICERS.

CHAPTER I.

OF THE CITY ATTORNEY.

[Ordinance Approved June 27th, 1870.]

SECTION 1. It shall be the duty of the City Attorney to give to the Common Council, any Committee thereof, the Mayor, Controller or any Board of the City, when requested, his legal counsel and opinion on all legal questions arising under, or concerning the charter or any ordinance of the City, and on all legal questions and subjects in which said City shall be legally interested. General powers and duties.

SEC. 2. The legal opinions of the City Attorney shall be given in writing, when they are reported to the Common Council, they shall be printed and published as part of the proceedings of the meeting of said Council at which they are reported, and when they are reported to any Committee, to the Mayor or officer of the City, they shall be filed by such committee, Mayor or officer of the City, in their office or in the office of the City Clerk. Opinions to be in writing when printed and filed.

SEC. 3. He shall appear as Attorney and Counsel in behalf of the City, in all suits, prosecutions or proceedings which shall be brought in the Recorder's Court, or any Circuit Court, or in the When he shall appear as Attorney and Counsellor.

Supreme Court of this State, or in any United States Court, by or against said City, or any officer thereof, or which, when thus brought, shall be removed in any mode whatever, from such Recorder's Court, Circuit Court, into the Supreme Court, as the case may require, shall prosecute or defend therein to the termination thereof.

Opening streets.

SEC. 4. He shall also act as the Attorney of the City, in the Recorder's Court, in all matters brought under the provisions of title 4, City Charter, in opening, altering, extending or closing streets, &c , and shall also act as the Attorney in all such suits, prosecutions and proceedings when in any manner removed to the Supreme Court.

When in behalf of officers of City.

SEC. 5. He shall, whenever directed by the Common Council, appear as Attorney and Counsel in behalf of any officer of the City, in any suit, prosecution or other judicial proceedings brought by or against such officer, in his official character; and as the case may require, shall prosecute and defend them to the termination thereof.

As member of Committee.

SEC. 6. He shall also act as a member of any Committee of the Common Council, and discharge the duties of a member thereof whenever directed by said Council.

To certify to bonds, deeds, leases, &c.

SEC. 7. He shall certify to the correctness of the form of all official bonds, deeds, leases and contracts of any kind in which the city is interested, before the same shall be accepted or adopted by the Common Council or any officer of the City.

Prepare draft of Ordinances & bills when requested.

SEC. 8. He shall also prepare and report to the Common Council, upon their request, the draft of any ordinance of the City, or bill to amend the charter of the City, to be presented to the Legislature.

To make report of suits.

SEC. 9. He shall on the first Monday in April of each year make a report in writing to the Common Council, duly verified by his oath, of all suits, prosecutions or actions prosecuted or defended by him during the preceeding year, of the names of the parties thereto, of the title of the courts in which they were commenced, of their progress or final disposition, and all other information concerning the legal interest of the City, which he may deem necessary or proper.

SEC. 10. The City Attorney shall be appointed by the Common Council, and shall hold his office for the term of one year; he shall be a practicing attorney of the Supreme Court of this State, and of good standing, as such; he shall keep his office in some public and convenient place in the City of East Saginaw, and shall before entering upon the duties of his office, give an official bond, with sureties, that he will faithfully discharge the duties of his office, in the penal sum of one thousand dollars.

Appointment and term of office. To give bonds, etc.

SEC. 11. He shall keep in a proper book, to be provided by the City for the purpose, a register of all actions, prosecutions and proceedings, prosecuted or defended by him, and of the various doings therein; and on the expiration of his official term, he shall forthwith, on demand, deliver to his successor in office such register, together with all deeds, cases, contracts or other papers and writings in his possession, delivered to him by or belonging to the City or any officer thereof, or any committee of the Common Council and shall also deliver a written consent of substitution of his successor in all such actions, prosecutions or proceedings, then pending and undetermined.

To keep a Register and deliver papers, etc., to his successor

---

CHAPTER II.

OF THE CITY MARSHAL AND HIS ASSISTANTS.

[Ordinance Approved July 11th, 1870.]

SECTION 1. The Marshal, Assistant Marshal and Constables, as conservators of the peace, shall possess and exercise the duties of township constables, under the General Laws of the State of Michigan.

Powers and duties.

SEC. 2. The Marshal and his Assistants shall serve all writs and processes of the Recorder's Court, in cases arising under the Ordinances, and in proceedings under the Charter for opening and extending streets, alleys, &c., making public improvements and enforcing the By-Laws and Ordinances of the city.

To serve process.

SEC. 3. The Marshal and his Assistants shall obey and execute all lawful precepts and commands of the Mayor, the Recorder's Court, the Common Council and the Board of Health of the City.

To obey and execute precepts.

To attend sessions of Recorder's Court, Common Council and Board of Health.

SEC. 4. The Marshal and his Assistants shall attend the sessions of the Recorder's Court, when engaged in trials and proceedings under the Charter and Ordinances, and also the sessions of the Common Council and the Board of Health.

To serve all notices relating to business of City, etc.

SEC. 5. The Marshal and his Assistants shall serve all papers and notices relating to the business of the city, which may be delivered to them by the Mayor, an Alderman, a member of the Board of Health, the Controller, Treasurer, City Attorney, or City Clerk.

To keep an office, etc.

SEC. 6. The Marshal and his Assistants shall keep their office in the place provided by the Common Council, and one of them shall be found in their office each day between the hours of 9 A. M. and 12 noon, and between the hours of 2 and 4 P. M., unless engaged elsewhere on public business.

To be Chief of Police, etc.

SEC. 7. The Marshal shall be the Chief of Police of the city and all Constables, Watchmen and Policemen, whether general or special, shall be subordinate to him and under his direction, subject, nevertheless, to the orders of the Mayor.

To make rules subject to the approval of the Mayor.

SEC. 8. The Marshal shall, subject to the approval of the Mayor, have power to make rules and regulations for the government of his Assistants and for the Constables, Watchmen and Policemen, when acting under his command, who are hereby required to obey the same. He may direct or deputise any Assistant Marshal to perform any duty which he himself might perform.

When on duty to wear uniform.

SEC. 9. The Marshal, Assistant Marshals, Watchmen and Policemen shall, when on duty, wear a blue coat with brass buttons, blue pantaloons and a hat, all to be of uniform style and fashion, and shall carry his police baton fastened in a belt or sash to be worn about the waist.

To aid in the suppression of crimes, etc.

SEC. 10. The Marshal, Assistant Marshals, Watchmen and Policemen shall aid in the suppression of crimes and misdemeanors, and it is hereby made their duty to arrest summarily all persons guilty of any violation of law of the City ordinances, and make complaint for the same before the Recorder or a Justice of the Peace of said City.

SEC. 11. The neglect or refusal of the Marshal, Assistant Marshal, a Constable, Watchman or Policeman, or either of them to perform any of the duties prescribed by the laws of this State, or by the Charter or any Ordinance of the City, or to make complaint for any violation of law or ordinance which may come to his or their knowledge, shall be considered a wilful neglect of the duties of his or their office, and be deemed a sufficient cause for his or their removal from office by the Mayor or Common Council.

Neglect or refusal of Marshal, etc. to perform duties prescribed, etc., cause for removal

SEC. 12. The Marshal, Assistant Marshal, Watchman or Policeman shall not be interested, either directly or indirectly, in the keeping of any tavern, saloon, barroom, coffee or entry house, or beer hall, or place of resort or amusement, in said city.

Not to be interested in keeping tavern, etc.

SEC. 13. No person shall be appointed Marshal, Assistant Marshal, Watchman or Policeman unless he has arrived at the age of twenty-one years and is of good moral character and temperate habits; and any officer named in this section, and any Constable who shall be guilty of any drunkeness, lewd or improper conduct, shall be removed from office by the Mayor or Common Council.

Qualifications for appointment.

SEC. 14. The Marshal shall have charge of the city prison and the prisoners in the same, and shall keep them himself, or by some suitable person for whose acts he shall be responsible; he shall be liable to the same extent for and possess the same powers in the safe keeping of prisoners confined in said prison, as keepers of county jails under the general laws of this State. He shall provide prisoners with proper and wholesome food, and keep the City prison in good repair, and in a cleanly and orderly condition; and he shall report to the Common Council, on the first Monday of each month, the names of all persons confined in said prison, the month previous; how and for what arrested; the cause and length of time of detention or arrest; the time of discharge from arrest or detention, and how and by whose authority.

Marshal to have charge of the City Prison, and his duties therein.

SEC. 15. No officer mentioned in this ordinance shall imprison or confine any person, except upon a lawful order of some competent court or officer, unless the arrest is made in the night time, or when there is no court or proper officer, before whom such pri-

Officers not to imprison or confine persons, except in certain cases, and under certain conditions.

soner can be brought, and in such case the person so arrested shall be brought before the proper court or officer at the earliest possible and practicable time—and complaint be made, and trial had in accordance with law and the ordinances of this City; nor shall any such officer discharge any person confined in the City prison, except upon a legal order of some court authorized to make such order.

To attend fires.

SEC. 16. The Marshal, Assistant Marshals and Constables shall attend all fires, and assist in extinguishing the same, and in preserving, removing and securing property, keep away and remove from fires all idle, disorderly or suspicious persons, and for such purpose may arrest in the discharge of such duty and temporarily confine any such disorderly or suspicious persons, and shall perform such other duties as are or may be prescribed or directed by the Charter or any Ordinance or resolution of the Common Council.

To give bonds.

SEC. 17. The officers named in this Ordinance shall each, before entering upon the duties of their respective offices, execute a Bond to the City of East Saginaw, in the penal sum of one thousand dollars, with one or more sureties, conditional for the faithful discharge of the duties of their office, and shall also subscribe the oath of office. The bond and oath of office shall be filed in the office of the City Clerk.

Penalty.

SEC. 18. Any violation of the provisions of this Ordinance, in addition to any other penalty therein provided, shall be punished by a fine not exceeding one hundred dollars and costs of prosecution, and in the imposition of any fine and costs, the court may make a further sentence that the offender be imprisoned until payment thereof: *Provided, however,* That such imprisonment shall not exceed the period of ninety days.

SEC. 19. That an Ordinance, entitled, "An Ordinance relative to the powers and duties of the Marshal, Assistant Marshal and Police Constables," be and the same is hereby repealed.

CHAPTER III.

OF THE CITY PHYSICIAN.

[Ordinance Approved July 11th, 1870.]

SECTION 1. There shall be appointed by the Common Council at their third regular meeting in the month of April and every year thereafter, one Physician, to be called the "City Physician," and who shall be of good standing in his profession, and shall possess and exercise the duties hereinafter prescribed. Appointment, powers and duties.

SEC. 2. It shall be the duty of the City Physician, when directed by the Mayor and Aldermen, or Director of the Poor, to attend any sick, disabled or infirm person who may be a charge upon the City, and render such medical assistance as may be necessary; also, when any City pauper is taken to the pest house or hospital, the Physician shall attend on the person so taken: *Provided*, in all cases of service in small pox cases, nothing in the ordinance shall be construed to prevent the City Physician from charging and collecting the usual fees against any person or persons, not a City pauper, or from receiving said fees in services rendered to persons who are a county charge. To attend sick in certain cases, etc.

SEC. 3. It shall be the duty of the City Physician to vaccinate without charge any inhabitant of the City of East Saginaw, not previously vaccinated, who may apply to him for that purpose; he shall also give certificates of vaccination to all persons vaccinated by him. To vaccinate without charge.

SEC. 4. The City Physician shall furnish at his own expense, all medicines which may be necessary in the skilful and proper treatment of such sick or disabled persons as may be a charge upon the City; and also such vaccine matters as may be required to carry into force the provisions of Section 3 of this Ordinance, but such City Physician shall be entitled, upon his affidavit, that he has vaccinated, free of charge all inhabitants of the City of East Saginaw, who have called upon him for that purpose, the sum of twenty dollars in addition to the salary of his office. To furnish medicines.

SEC. 5. It shall be the duty of the City Clerk to procure, at the expense of the City, suitable cards, upon which shall be Name and residence to be published printed a copy of Section 3 of this Ordinance, and also the name and residence of the City Physician; such card shall be placed and kept in conspicuous positions in the office of the City Physician and in the offices of the Treasurer, City Clerk, City Marshal and Diretor of the Poor.

Must have received diploma from medical college.

SEC. 6. No person shall be eligible to the office of City Physician who has not received a diploma from a respectable medical college.

Complaints against.

SEC. 7. All complaints against the City Physician shall be made in writing to the Mayor, who shall investigate the same, and if necessary, report the case to the Common Council, with his opinion thereon.

Substitute in case of absence.

SEC. 8. In case of the absence or inability, from any cause, of the City Physician to attend the duties of the office, he shall, with the consent of the Mayor, provide a competent Physician to fill his place.

CHAPTER IV.

OF THE CITY CLERK.

[Ordinance Approved August 1st, 1870.]

Appointm't, how made.

SECTION 1. That on the third regular meeting of the Common Council, in the month of April in each year, or as soon thereafter as may be, and as often as any vacancy shall occur there shall be appointed, by ballot, a City Clerk, who shall hold his office for one year; and until his successor is duly appointed and qualified.

May appoint a Deputy.

SEC. 2. He may appoint a Deputy Clerk, whose acts he shall be responsible for.

His duties.

SEC. 3. Said Clerk shall keep an accurate and correct journal of the proceedings of the Council; he shall have the custody of all the laws and ordinances of the city, and also the corporate seal. It shall be his duty to see that all the ordinances are promptly and correctly published in the official paper of the city, and such other papers as may be directed by the Council; he shall furnish all transcripts, orders and certificates called for by any person, and authenticate the same by his official signature under the seal of the corporation.

SEC. 4. For all attested transcripts, orders and certificates, other than those ordered by the Common Council, the same fees shall be paid as are allowed to the Clerk of the Circuit Court for similar services. He shall receive such other pay and perform such other duties proper to his office as the Council shall, from time to time, order and cetermine. Fees in certain cases.

SEC. 5. The City Clerk shall, before entering upon the duties of his office, execute and file a bond with sureties, to be approved by the Common Council, for the faithful performance of the duties of his office, and the said keeping of papers and all records therein, and the transfer of the same to his successor. Such bonds shall be in such principal sums as the Common Council shall direct, not less than five thousand dollars, and shall be deposited with the City Controller for safe keeping. Bond.

CHAPTER V.

OF THE CITY SURVEYOR.

[Ordinance Approved June 27th, 1870.]

SECTION 1. It shall be the duty of the City Surveyor, when so directed by the Common Council, to ascertain and establish the proper grade to any avenue, street, lane, alley or sidewalk within the limits of said City, and when required, to run out and stake off the same. City Surveyor to establish grade of streets.

SEC. 2. It shall also be his duty to keep an office in said City, to make all necessary surveys, and superintend the construction, enlargement or alteration of all drains, connecting with the main, or lateral sewers in said City, and shall record the same in a book or books to be provided by the Common Council, and keep the same in his office, and deliver the same to his successor at the termination of his term of office. To survey and superintend the construction or alteration of drains and make report.

SEC. 3. In shall also be his duty to make all necessary plans and specifications in the stumping, ditching and grading of any street in said City, in opening, extending or widening any street, and he shall superintend, direct and certify to the execution of To make all plans and specificat'ns as for streets all work by contract for such purposes in said City. He shall keep a record of the same and all facts connected therewith neccessary to protect the interests of the City and deliver the same to his successor in office.

To make surveys and give information to officers of City, etc.

Sec. 4. He shall also make all necessary surveys, and give such information as may be needed by any city officer or committee of the Common Council, and shall at all times, when required, consult and act with any standing or special committee who may desire any information or assistance in any matter or thing connected with the duties of his office, where the City of East Saginaw is a party interested.

To keep in his office all plans and drafts relating to surveys, etc.

Sec. 5. He shall keep in his office, subject to proper public uses, all plans and drafts relating to any survey made by order of the Common Council, and shall also make a written report of his doings and proceedings in all cases when required so to do by the Common Council.

Salery. To deliver books and papers to his successor.

Sec. 6. The salary allowed by said Common Council to the City Surveyor, shall be in full for all services rendered, and shall also be in full for all incidental as well as other labor performed by him as said Surveyor, or for any of his assistants. All maps, plats, profiles, estimates and surveys made by order of the Common Council, and paid for by the City shall be public property, to be properly recorded and filed in the Surveyor's office, and shall be delivered to his successor in office as the property of said City.

Bond.

Sec. 7. Before entering upon the duties of his office, the City Surveyor shall make and file a bond, with sureties to be approved by the Council, in the sum of not less than one thousand dollars, conditioned for the faithful performance of the duties of said office.

CHAPTER VI.

OF THE STREET COMMISSIONER.

[Ordinance Approved May 8th, 1865.]

SECTION 1. The Street Commissioner, under the direction of the Common Council, shall take charge of and superintend all constructions and repairs of sewers, drains, streets, lanes, alleys, crosswalks and sidewalks, bridges and culverts, and direct the cleaning and improvement of all streets and public places in the City. Street Commissioner to superintend construction of streets, etc., and cleaning of the same, etc.

SEC. 2. Whenever the Street Commissioner shall be directed by the Common Council, to do any of the work or labor specified in Section 1, he shall at the completion of the same make and file with the Controller a detailed and true statement of the amount of work performed and the cost of the same, and the cost and quality of the material used, the precise locality where done and the extent of the same, and that such work or labor has been performed in accordance with the ordinances of the city, or resolutions of the Common Council, as the case may be. Filing of statement of work, etc., with the City Controller.

SEC. 3. The Street Commissioner shall make and file with the Controller, on the first Monday of each month, from and including the month of May to and including the month of December, if he shall be employed for that time, a detailed statement of the amount of work performed and the cost of the same, together with the amount of property in his possession belonging to the City. To make monthly reports.

SEC. 4. Whenever the Common Council shall order the construction or repair of any sidewalk or crosswalk, the same shall be constructed or repaired and the expense shall be assessed by the Street Commissioner in accordance with the ordinance of the city relative to sidewalks and crosswalks, and the ordinances amendatory thereto, unless otherwise ordered. Power to assess.

SEC. 5. It shall be the duty of the Street Commissioner, to report to the Common Council from time to time the condition of the sidewalks and crosswalks, streets and alleys, sewers, culverts, drains and bridges within the City, and make such recommendations for the improvement of the same as he shall think for the best interest of the city. To make occasional reports.

Oath and Bond.

SEC. 6. Before entering upon the duties of his office, the Street Commissioner shall take and subscribe the oath of office, and enter into a bond in the penal sum of one thousand dollars, with one or more sureties to be approved by the Common Council, conditioned for the faithful performance of the duties of his office.

[Ordinance Approved May 21st, 1866.]

Powers and duties more fully defined.

SECTION 1. The Street Commissioner shall have all the powers and perform all the duties prescribed to be performed by the City Marshal in any of the ordinances in force in this city, except the collection of taxes and assessments, and except the duties of the Marshal as chief of police, police constable, attendance upon courts and service of process issued by a court, the care of the city jail and persons confined therein, and shall enforce all ordinances relative to the repairing and cleaning streets, sidewalks, crosswalks, nuisances and obstruction of streets.

CHAPTER VII.

OF THE CITY CONTROLLER.

[Ordinance Approved May 8th, 1865.]

Countersigning bonds.

SECTION 1. The Controller shall constitute the chief financial officer of the corporation, and as such, shall countersign all bonds which the corporation or Common Council are authorized to issue, pledging the faith and credit of the city.

Examinat'n of claims and dema'ds against the City.

SEC. 2. All claims and demands against the city shall be referred to the Controller, who shall examine the same in detail, and present the same to the Common Common Council at their next regular meeting, or as soon thereafter as practicable, together with a communication in writing, setting forth the facts in relation to such claims and demands, and his opinion in regard to the payment thereof.

Power to purchase personal propertyand supplies for the use of the City.

SEC. 3. The Controller shall, under the direction of the Common Council, make all purchases of personal property, supplies and materials required for the use of the City in its various departments, and report his action therein from time to time to the Common Council, or as may be required by them.

SEC. 4. The Controller shall examine the tax rolls and returns of the Marshal. The reports and returns of the City Treasurer and Street Commissioner, and of all other City officers involving receipts or expenditures of moneys or values connected with the City, and report in writing as to the correctness of the same to the Common Council from time to time or as may be required by the Council.

Power to examine the tax rolls and returns of the Marshal and the reports and returns of all other City Officers involving expenditures of money, to report such examinati'n to Common Council.

SEC. 5. The Controller shall keep a complete set of books exhibiting the financial condition of the corporation in all its various departments, and funds, its resources and liabilities with a proper classification thereof. When any fund or appropriation has been exhausted by warrants already drawn thereon, or by appropriations, liabilities, debts and expenses actually made, incurred or contracted for and to be paid out of such funds or appropriations, the Controller shall advise the Common Council of the situation thereof at its next regular meeting.

Duty to keep a complete set of books exhibiting the financial condition of corporation in all its various departments. Place of office.

He shall open accounts with the Marshal and Treasurer, charging them with the amount of taxes, General and Special, levied in the corporation, specified in the tax rolls delivered to them; also, the whole amount in detail of all bonds, notes, mortgages and money receivable of the corporation. He shall keep a list of all the property, real, personal and mixed, belonging to the City to the end that the assets and liabilities of the corporation may at any time be known at the Controller's office, which shall be kept at or adjacent to the Common Council rooms.

SEC. 6. The Controller shall at the request of the Street Commissioner and under his direction, and also at the request of Special Commissioners or Jury, and under their direction make and extend all assessments, rolls for special assessments and public improvements which may be ordered by the Common Council.

Powers to extend assessment roll for special assessment and public improvem't.

SEC. 7. The Assistant Controller may do and perform all acts mentioned in this ordinance under the liability of City Charter viz: that the Controller shall be responsible for his acts.

Power of Assistant Controller.

CHAPTER VIII.

OF THE CITY ASSESSOR.

[Ordinance Approved July 18th, 1870.]

Appointm't, term of office, etc.

SECTION 1. The City Assessor shall be appointed by the Common Council, and shall hold his office for the term of three years, as provide in section 6, of title 4, of the City Charter, and shall devote his whole time, when necessary, to the services of the City in connection with the duties of his office.

Oath and bond.

SEC. 2. Before entering upon the duties of his office, the Assessor shall take and subscribe the oath provided by the City Charter, and shall execute a bond to the corporation with one or more sufficient sureties, in the sum of ten thousand dollars, conditioned that he will faithfully perform the duties of his office, and on demand deliver over to his successor, or other proper officer or agent of the corporation, all books, papers, moneys, effects and property belonging to the corporation or appertaining to his office.

To assess property and make assessment rolls.

SEC. 3. The Assessor shall, between the first day of January and May in each year, in the manner provided by the City Charter, assess all the real and personal property subject to assessment or taxation within the several wards of the City, and within the same period shall make out and complete the assessment rolls for said City in proper books to be provided for that purpose.

To keep assessment rolls, etc.

SEC. 4. The Assessor shall keep in his office complete sets of all assessment rolls, made by him and confirmed by the Common Council, and all books, rolls and records in his office shall be open to public inspection. The City Assessment rolls, when not in use by the Treasurer or Controller, shall be kept in said Assessor's office, and he shall be responsible for the proper keeping of the same, and all other records required by the charter to be placed in his keeping.

May require the assistance of City Surveyor.

SEC. 5. The Assessor may require the services of the City Surveyor, in ascertaining the divisions and boundaries or any real estate within the City; and it is hereby made the duty of said Surveyor to render such services whenever applied to by the Assessor.

SEC. 6. The Controller shall procure for the Assessor all stationery, books or printing for the City; such books, stationery and printing as he may from time to time require for his office, and the same shall be paid for by the City of East Saginaw. Controller to procure stationary for

SEC. 7. The Assessor shall prepare the tax rolls for highway, sewer, school and City taxes, of each ward in the city, and deliver the same, when completed, to the Controller; he shall also prepare the tax rolls for State and County taxes for each ward in the City, as required by law, and deliver the same when the taxes are extended thereon to the City Controller. To prepare tax rolls.

SEC. 8. The Assessor shall carefully preserve and keep all books, papers and records appertaining to or filed in his office, and deliver the same to his lawful successor. To preserve books, etc.

CHAPTER IX.

OF WARD COLLECTORS.

[Ordinance Approved July 25th, 1870.]

SECTION 1. The Collector of each Ward shall collect all State and County Taxes assessed and imposed upon the real and personal property of such ward, and all such City, highway, sewer and school taxes and special assessment rolls as shall be placed in their hands for collection by the Controller or other proper officer of said City. Ward Collector to collect State and County taxes, etc.

SEC. 2. The penalty of the bond of each Ward Collector given to the said City, for the faithful performance of his duties, shall be in a sum at least double the amount of the taxes placed in his hands for collection on personal property of the ward for which he is elected or appointed, and in such further sum as the Common Council may by resolution direct. Bond.

SEC. 3. It shall be the duty of each Collector during the time he has any tax roll in his hands for collection of City taxes, on Monday of each week, to deposit with the Treasurer all sums of money collected by him during the week and since his last deposit, for which sums he shall take the Treasurer's receipt in duplicate, one of which he shall within twenty-four hours after To pay over money to Treasurer and file statement.

receiving the same, file with the Controller of the City with the statements required by the charter, and shall at the same time file with the Controller a statement in writing, that the amount so deposited by him with said Treasurer, was all the money belonging to the City, collected by him, and in his possession at the time of making said deposit, which statement shall be signed by the Collector making the same, and sworn to by him before the Controller, who shall report to the Common Council the failure of any Collector to comply with this ordinance; but in case any Collector shall not have collected any money during the seven days, then he shall report the fact to the Treasurer and shall make a sworn statement of the same to the Controller.

May levy upon and sell property

SEC. 4. It shall be the duty of the Collectors to collect from the persons named in their respective Assessment rolls, the assessment or tax therein specified and set forth as due from such persons, and for such purposes they may levy upon and sell the personal property of any kind or description of any person liable to pay and refusing or neglecting to do so, and any Collector may levy upon the property of such person wherever the same may be found in the City of East Saginaw.

Penalty for resisting levy, etc.

SEC. 5. Any person or persons who shall resist, obstruct or hinder any Ward Collector of said City in levying upon or taking into possession any goods and chattels under and by virtue of a warrant legally issued and directed to said Ward Collector, for the collection of any tax or assessment of said City. Said goods and chattels being legally liable to be so levied on and taken into possession by said Ward Collector, shall be punished by a fine not exceeding one hundred dollars or by imprisonment not to exceed ninety days or by both such fine and imprisonment in the discretion of the Court.

Penalty for resisting entry of collector.

SEC. 6. Any person who shall prevent any Ward Collector from entering upon any house or premises occupied by him or her for the purpose of searching for or levying on goods and chattels under any warrant legally issued for the collection of tax or assessment which the person so occupying said house or premises is liable to pay, shall be punished by the same fine or imprisonment or by both, in the discretion of the court, as is provided in the preceeding section.

CHAPTER X.

OF THE DIRECTOR OF THE POOR.

[Ordinance Approved June 27th, 1870.]

SECTION 1 Before entering upon the duties of his office, the Director of the Poor shall execute a bond to the City of East Saginaw, in the penal sum of five thousand dollars, with one or more sufficient sureties, conditioned, that he will faithfully discharge the duties of his office, and fulfill the requirements of this ordinance. Bond.

SEC. 2. The Director of the Poor shall keep his office in a suitable and convenient place in the City of East Saginaw, and keep the same open during usual business hours each day, (Sundays excepted). Office and office hours.

SEC. 3. It shall be the duty of the Director of the Poor, when any person, claiming to be a City pauper, shall by himself or another apply to him for relief, to make immediate personal inquiry into the state and circumstances of the applicant, and if it shall appear that he or she is in such indigent circumstances as to require permanent support, and is lawfully a City charge, and is not so sick, diseased, lame or otherwise disabled, that he or she cannot safely or conveniently be removed, to remove such person to the County poor house, to be relieved and cared for as their necessities may require; but if such person cannot be safely and conveniently removed for any of the reasons herein before specified, the Director of the Poor shall report the same to the Mayor and Controller, and may afford such persons relief under the provisions of this ordinance, as the Mayor, Controller and Director of the Poor may jointly agree and authorize, until such time as he or she can be removed to the County poor house; and if it shall appear that any person applying for relief as aforesaid, requires only temporary relief or partial support, he shall, with the consent of the Mayor and Controller as above set forth, afford him or her such relief as the circumstances of the case may require. Whenever from sickness or other disability the Director of the Poor shall deem it necessary and proper to place any City pauper in Duties and powers.

the City hospital; he, shall do so by removing such pauper to said hospital, and shall report such action in writing to the Controller, giving the name, age, residence, disease and other proper information in such report, and the board and care of such pauper shall be paid for in the same manner as other claims and demands against the corporation.

Supplies for support of poor.

SEC. 4. The Director of the Poor shall, on or before the first Monday in October in each and every year, report to the Controller the quantity of wood, flour, groceries, meats, articles of clothing, and such other articles as in his judgment may be necessary for the support of the poor, for the ensuing year; such estimate to be based upon the quantity of such articles used for that purpose during the preceding year. Within twenty days after the receipt of such report, the Controller shall advertise for at least ten days in one or more newspapers, published in this city, for sealed proposals to furnish and supply so many and such quantity of the articles enumerated in the report of the Director of the Poor, as the City may require; such articles to be delivered at convenient places in the City of East Saginaw, and in such quantities as the City may from time to time require. Such supplies may be kept under the control of, or in the office of the Director of the Poor, in such quantities as the Mayor and Controller shall direct, and it shall be the duty of the Director of the Poor to account for the same to the Mayor and Controller, as they may be drawn from the Contractor at such times and in such quantities as needed upon the order of the said Director of the Poor.

When to give orders for supplies and money.

SEC. 5. It shall be the duty of the Director of the Poor, when any person, being a City pauper, shall apply to him for relief, and the Mayor, Controller and Director of the Poor shall determine his or her state and circumstances are such as to render relief necessary and proper to give such person such proper relief, either from the supplies belonging to the City on hand, or by giving an order on the contractor or contractors furnishing the article or articles needed by such person. In any case where the Mayor, Controller and Director of the Poor shall deem it for the best interest of the City to furnish pecuniary aid to any pauper, the Director of the Poor shall give such pauper a certificate for the amount which he may deem necessary; and the Treasurer, upon the presentation to him of such certificate, shall pay the same, and present his account and voucher therefor to the Controller, to be audited and allowed by the Common Council, as other claims against the City, and when so allowed, the warrant shall be used by the Treasurer to balance the payment as made, and for no other purpose.

SEC. 6. The Common Council shall from time to time, upon the report of the Controller, that an appropriation is necessary for the purpose, appropriate out of the poor fund limited sums, to be subject to the orders of the Director of the Poor, to meet the cases provided for in the preceding section. Common Council to appropriate funds.

SEC. 7. It shall be the duty of the contractors furnishing supplies to the city for the purposes herein before specified, to present to the Controller on the first of every month, a monthly account of supplies furnished by him, together with all orders which shall have been drawn upon him by the Director of the Poor, which account shall be accompanied by an affidavit as required by section 18, title 5 of the City Charter, and shall be audited and allowed like all other claims and demands against the City, and paid out of the poor fund. Contractors for supplies, how to be furnished.

SEC. 8 It shall be the duty of the Director of the Poor, to give to paupers needing medical aid, an order therefor on the City Physician. Medical aid to Poor.

SEC 9. It shall be the duty of the Controller to procure railroad tickets for paupers who may wish permanently to leave the State, when recommended to do so by the Director of the Poor. Railroad tickets to paupers leaving the State.

SEC. 10. It shall be the duty of the Director of the Poor to immediately report to the Common Council all cases of insane or foolish persons who may become a City charge; also all cases of diseases of the eye, or other affliction which he has reason to believe can be cured by skilful or surgical treatment, and to carry out and execute any orders the Common Council may make in reference thereto. Director to report to the Council in certain cases.

SEC. 11. A failure or wilful neglect to obey this ordinance, and faithfully discharge the duties of the office, shall subject the incumbent for removal or prosecution for misdemeanor, as provided in the amendatory act to the act to incorporate the City of East Saginaw, approved March 16th, 1869. Failure to neglect to obey, etc.

CHAPTER XI.

OF INSPECTOR OF FIRE WOOD.

[Ordinance Approved December 17th, 1866.]

Common Council may appoint Wood Inpector.

SECTION 1. There shall be appointed by the Common Council once in each year, an Inspector of Fire Wood, who shall hold his office for one year, unless sooner lawfully removed, who shall have the power to appoint one or more Assistants to be paid by himself and who shall perform the duties herein provided and be responsible for the acts and omissions of said Assistants.

All wood offered for sale must be inspected by the Wood Inspector.

SEC. 2. No person shall sell or offer for sale within the limits of the City, or deliver within the limits of the City, any firewood, without having the same measured and inspected by the City Inspector of Wood or one of his Assistants, and obtaining a certificate of inspection and measurement of the same.

SEC. 3. When requested by the buyer or Inspector of Wood, or his Assistants, the person delivering wood shall pile or cause to be piled the same in a compact and square form and as directed by the Inspector.

Duty of Wood Inspector.

SEC. 4. It shall be the duty of the Inspector of Wood to carefully, promptly and impartially measure and inspect fire wood, (except as herein otherwise provided) and give a certificate of the same, which certificate shall be *prima facia* evidence of the facts therein contained between the buyer and seller, and for any violation of the duties of his office shall be removed by the Common Council and shall rseeive the following fees: For inspecting and measuring each load of wood, ten cents, and five cents for each certificate given.

Penalty.

SEC. 5. Any person who shall violate any of the provisions of this ordinance, shall, on conviction thereof in any court of competent jurisdiction, be fined not less than five dollars nor more than twenty-five dollars, and on failure to pay the fine or penalty imposed, shall be imprisoned in the county jail of Saginaw county, or the City prison for any term not exceeding ten days.

SEC. 6. This ordinance shall not apply to wood delivered under contract in a quantity of not less than three cords, when by the terms of the contract such wood is to be piled for measurement.

SEC. 7. The ordinance entitled "An Ordinance concerning the inspection and measurement of fire wood, made and passed the first day of February, 1864, is hereby repealed. Made and passed by the Common Council of the City of East Saginaw, this, the seventeenth day of December, 1866.

CHAPTER XII.

OF THE CITY SCAVENGER.

[Ordinance Approved July 11th, 1870.]

SECTION 1. No person shall follow the business or occupation of Scavenger without authority of the Common Council, and a proper license therefor. Scavengers must be licensed.

SEC. 2. The Common Council may appoint one or more proper persons to act as Scavengers. Before entering upon the duties of their office, they shall execute a bond to the city in the sum of fifty dollars, with one or more sufficient sureties, conditional, for the faithful observance of the charter and this ordinance. Appointm't and bond.

SEC. 3. Such Scavengers, under the direction of the Mayor, Chief of Police, or of the Board of Health, shall be authorized and have the right to enter upon any premises in said City, between sunrise and sunset, and examine any vault, sink, privy or private drain. Power to enter on premises and examine sink, etc.

SEC. 4. Whenever in the opinion of the Mayor, Chief of Police or the Board of Health, any sink, privy or private drain shall need cleansing, altering, relaying or repairing, in order to protect the public health, they shall have the same examined, and if such necessity exists, notify, in writing, the owner or occupant thereof to cause the same to be cleansed, altered, relaid or repaired, within six days from the date of the services of such notice, and in case of the neglect or refusal of any owner or occupant so notified to comply with the requirements of such notice, the Common Council may direct the proper officer to cleanse, alter, relay or repair such sink, private drain or privy, and assess the expenses thereof on the lot or premises on which the same is situate or be- How sinks, etc., to be cleansed, altered or repaired—Assessment of expenses thereof.

longs, which assessment shall be a lien on such lot or premises, and be collected in the manner as other assessments imposed by authority of the Common Council, and provided for in section nine, title ten of the City Charter.

Sinks, etc. to be emptied in tight and covered boxes.

SEC. 5. Scavengers shall not empty or remove the contents of any tub, vault, sink, privy or private drain, otherwise than in boxes or casks made tight and closely covered.

Scavengers to clean the sinks, etc., and remove nuisances when requested.

SEC. 6. Whenever requested by the owner or occupant of any premises in writing, the Scavenger shall cleanse or empty any vault, sink, private drain or privy, and remove any and all nuisances from such premises. The Scavengers may demand and receive their fees for such services in advance.

Fees of Scavengers.

SEC. 7. The Scavengers shall receive ten cents for each cubic foot of the contents of any sink, private drain or vault, by them cleaned out or removed; for removing and burrying any horse, mule, cow or cattle, five dollars each; and for removing any dead dog, hog or similar animal, one dollar each; for removing other nuisance, they shall receive such fees as may from time to time be fixed by resolution of the Common Council, or agreed upon between the parties in interest.

Penalty.

SEC. 8. Any violation of, or neglect, or refusal to comply with the provisions of this ordinance, shall be punished by a fine not to exceed twenty-five dollars and costs of suit, and in the imposition of any fine and costs, the court may make a further sentence that the offender may be imprisoned until the payment thereof: *Provided*, the term of such imprisonment shall not exceed the period of thirty days.

CHAPTER XIII.

OF INSPECTOR OF GAS METERS

[Ordinance Approved Oct. 24th, 1870.]

Appointm't and term of office.

SECTION 1. There shall be an officer in the City of East Saginaw, to be denominated "The Inspector of Gas Meters," with the powers and duties hereinafter prescribed, to be appointed by the Common Council, and to hold his office for one year, or until his successor is appointed.

SEC. 2. The Inspector of Gas Meters shall receive such salary per annum as the Common Council shall by resolution direct, to be paid by the East Saginaw Gas Light Company or the City of East Saginaw, in equal monthly payments, as the Common Council may deem advisable. Salary.

SEC. 3. Before entering upon the duties of his office, the Inspector of Gas Meters shall execute a Bond to the City of East Saginaw, in the penal sum of one thousand dollars, with two sureties conditional for the faithful discharge of the duties of his office, and of this Ordinance, and shall also take and subscribe the oath of office. The bond and oath shall be filed in the office of the City Clerk. Bond.

SEC. 4. He shall keep his office in a room to be provided by the Common Council, where he shall be found at all convenient hours of the day. Office.

SEC. 5. He shall keep in his office a good and accurate standard photometer, meter and prover to be furnished by the City of East Saginaw. To keep photometer, etc.

SEC. 6. Whenever requested, he shall examine and test, without charge, any meter furnished by the Gas Company, which may be brought to his office, and shall give notice to the consumer and the Gas Company, of the time when any meter is to be examined and tested, and after testing and proving any meter, he shall duly stamp the same. To test meters.

SEC. 7. His inspection shall be conclusive upon both the Gas Company and the consumer, as to the accuracy of any meter; and whenever any meter shall be found to be imperfect or inaccurate, it shall be replaced by the Gas Company with a good and sufficient meter. Inspection to be conclusive.

SEC. 8. It is hereby made the duty of the Inspector of Gas Meters, to keep a supervision over the public lamps of the City and see that they are kept clean, and at all times provided with good and sufficient burners of equal size; he shall at the end of each month examine the public meters and make a record of the number of feet of gas indicated by such meters, and shall compare the same with the bill of gas presented to the City by the Gas Compnny. To supervise public lamps and meters.

To make and report tests. SEC. 9. The Inspector of Gas Meters shall from time to time make photometrical tests of the gas furnished by the Gas Company, and shall communicate to the Common Council the result of such tests.

To make report. SEC. 10. He shall from time to time give the Common Council information of the condition of the public lamps of the City, and of the quantity of the gas furnished by the Gas Company.

To keep books. SEC. 11. He shall keep a book in his office, in which he shall record the number of each meter and the time when it was tested and proved by him, and such record shall be open at all times for public inspection.

May be suspended. SEC. 12. He may be suspended at any time by the Mayor, who shall report the same to the Common Council with his reason therefor, and shall be subject to removal at any time, by vote of the said Common Council.

CHAPTER XIV.

OF CHIEF OF POLICE, POLICE CONSTABLES AND WATCHMEN.

[Ordinance Approved October 24th, 1870.]

Duty of the Chief of Police, etc. SECTION 1. It shall be the duty of the Chief of Police, and of all Police Constables and Watchmen, whether on duty by day or night, to act under the action of the Mayor, and in conformity to the City ordinances. It is also made their duty to suppress all riots, disturbances and breaches of the peace, to apprehend any and all persons of the act of committing any offence against the laws of the State or ordinances of the City, and forthwith to bring such person before the Police Justice, a Justice of the Peace of the City or the Recorder's Court for examination. They may enter any house or building into which any person may flee; who has in their presence violated any law of the State, ordinance of the City, or into any house or building whence any noise, alarm or outcry may proceed. It is made their duty, upon reasonable information, to procure process for the arrest of any person charged with the breach of any City ordinance, and at all times faithfully and diligently to enforce all the ordinances of the City, and to perform all the duties imposed upon them by the charter.

SEC. 2. The Watchmen shall go on duty at six o'clock in the evening and remain on duty till five o'clock in in the morning. The Police Constables shall go on duty at five o'clock in the morning and remain on duty till six o'clock in the evening.

Time of duty of Watchmen and Police Constables.

SEC. 3. It shall be the duty of the Chief of Police, under the direction of the Mayor, to assign from week to week the Police Constables and Watchmen to their various beats, and it shall be his duty, at least twice in twenty-four hours, and as much oftener as possible, to visit each day and night beat in the city, and ascertain by personal inspection whether the Police Constables and Watchmen are doing their duty.

Duty of the Chief of Police.

SEC. 4. If any person or persons shall abuse, resist or obstruct the Chief of Police, any Police Constable or Watchman, in the exercise of his duties, the person or persons so offending shall, upon conviction thereof, be fined not less than five dollars nor more than thirty dollars, and in default of the payment of such fine shall be imprisoned in the county jail or City prison for a term not exceeding twenty days.

Penalty for resisting officers.

SEC. 5. All ordinances or parts of ordinances inconsistent with this ordinance are hereby repealed.

CHAPTER XV.

OF UNIFORMING POLICEMEN AND THEIR DUTIES IN CERTAIN CASES.

[Ordinance Approved September 16th, 1867.]

SECTION 1. That all Police Constables, Policemen, Watchmen and other members of the regular police force of this City, shall hereafter be required to procure and while on duty shall wear the following described uniform, to wit: Coat to be of dark blue cloth, single breasted, frock pattern, narrow standing collar, brass M. P. buttons, nine buttons in front and six on the skirts. Pants to be of dark blue cloth with light blue stripe on outer seams. Cap to be of dark blue cloth wide band large round top, leather frontis piece, leather half band and chin strap, fastened with small brass buttons.

Police Constables, etc., shall wear uniform.

Description of uniform.

Silver Star, club, belt, etc., to be furnished by City.

SEC. 2 Each member of the regular Police force, shall be furnished by the city with a silver Star, to be worn upon the left breast, numbers for the cap, club, belt and one pair of handcuffs, which shall be charged to him by the Chief of Police, to be returned when discharged and paid for at cost in case of loss or breakage unless such loss or breakage occurs in the discharge of duty and was unavoidable.

Uniform of Chief of Police.

SEC. 3. That the Chief of Police shall wear the uniform herein prescribed, except the number on the cap in place of which he shall wear a badge, on which shall be plainly marked or engraved the words "Chief of Police."

Mayor and Chief of Police to assign hours for duty, etc.

SEC. 4. That the Mayor and Chief of Police shall assign the numbers and hours for duty to the several members of the Police force of the city, regular and special, which shall be filed in the City Clerk's office, and in case of vacancy or dismissal, or the number of the force is increased or diminished, a new assignment of numbers shall be made and filed in the form following:

Police Register.

POLICE REGISTER.

HEADQUARTERS POLICE FORCE,
East Saginaw, Mich.——187-

THIS IS TO CERTIFY, That the following is the record of the regular Police force of the City of East Saginaw, as this day assigned and registered.

——— *Chief of Police.*

NAME.	NO.	WHEN APPOINTED.	HOURS FOR DUTY.	REMARKS.

And whenever it may be considered necessary by the Mayor or Common Council to appoint Special or additional Policemen or Watchmen, a similar list and assignment shall in all cases be made out and filed with the City Clerk.

SEC. 5. That every member of the Police force who shall appear upon duty without the uniform prescribed in this ordinance, shall be liable to a fine of five dollars for each offence. Penalty for appearing on duty without uniform.

SEC. 6. That any member of the Police force of this city, who shall, during the hours assigned him for duty, neglect the same, or who shall enter or resort to any saloon, shop, store, office or dwelling, except in the discharge of his duties, or who shall loiter or stand upon the street corners or sit upon boxes, awnings, steps or sidewalks, except when so ordered or stationed by the Mayor or Chief of Police, shall be liable to be suspended or discharged. To regulate the conduct of the Police force.

SEC. 7. That any member of the Police force, who shall violate any Ordinance of the City or any rules established for the regulation of the Police force, may be suspended by the Mayor and Chief of Police until the next meeting of the Common Council, and the Chief of Police shall, in all cases of suspension, at the next meeting of the Common Council, present written charges against the party so suspended for its action and advice, and the Common Council shall without delay enquire into such charges and pronounce judgment thereon, and no member of the Police force removed or discharged by the Common Council for neglect of duty or violation of the Ordinance of the City, shall be eligible to reappointment as regular or special Policeman or Watchman during the period of one year from the date of such dismissal. How dismissed.

SEC. 8. Every member of the Police force, when off duty, shall divest himself of his uniform and be dressed in citizen's clothing; except that he shall be required to wear his star as directed in Section 2, [as amended by Ordinance approved August 15th, 1870.] To wear citizen's clothes when off duty.

CHAPTER XVI.

OFFICE OF POLICE JUSTICE, CITY CONSTABLES AND CITY MARSHAL.

[Ordinance Approved April 24th, 1861.]

City Treasury or defendant's liable for fees.

Section 1. The following fees shall be allowed to officers hereinafter mentioned, for services hereafter rendered by them, to be paid out of the City Treasury, or by defendants convicted for the violation of any Ordinance of said City, or by complainants as the court before whom the case is tried may be adjudged.

Fees of Police Justices.

Sec. 2. The fees of Police Justices of the City of East Saginaw, for the services, hereinafter specified to be rendered by them shall be as follows: For administering every oath, 6 cents; for a summons, warrant or venire, thirteen cents; for a bond or recognizance, twenty-five cents; for a subpœna, thirteen cents, for each subpœna, not exceeding four in any one case; for commitment for want of bail, twenty-five cents; for any other services rendered by a Police Justice under the City Charter, the same fees as for similar services rendered by Justices of the Peace in this State in civil and criminal proceedings.

Provided, That, in all cases, when parties are brought before such Justice for violation of a City Ordinance without process, and a summary trial and conviction is had, the fees of such Justice shall be one dollar and twenty-five cents.

That in all cases under the Ordinances of this City, the said Justices shall, when the accused party is adjudged guilty, impose costs of the prosecution in addition to the penalty, and such costs shall be collected and paid the same as the penalty, and may be retained by the Justice.

Provided, That in no case shall the penalty and costs so imposed, exceed the penalty limited in the Ordinance for the violation of which such penalty is imposed. [*As amended by Ordinance approved July* 17, 1865.]

Fees of City Marshal, etc.

Sec. 3. The fees of the City Marshal and City Constables of the City of East Saginaw, for the services hereinafter specified to be rendered by them, shall be as follows.

For serving a warrant or other process for the arrest of any person, issued by any Police Justice, twenty-five cents; for traveling in the service of any process, 6 cents for each mile from the place of service to the place of return; for taking a defendant into custody on mitimus, twenty-five cents; for conveying a person before a magistrate or court before whom he is required to be brought, twenty-five cents; for serving a subpœna, thirteen cents for each witness and the like mileage as above provided, but mileage shall be allowed only on distance actually and necessarily traveled; for arresting and committing to the City Jail without warrant for any offence against the City Ordinances, fifty cents; *Provided*, that they shall, as soon as convenient, convey such person before some officer having jurisdiction of such offence and make a complaint against such person, and *Provided further*, that, if it shall appear on the trial, that he was committed without just cause, then no fees shall be allowed such Marshal or Constable for arresting, committing to jail or taking such person before the Magistrate or other officer.

For boarding prisoners in the City Jail, thirty-eight cents per day for the time such person is actually confined in said jail by warrant or mitimus or without process.

The Common Council of the City of East Saginaw, may allow such further compensation for service of process and the expense and trouble attending the same, as they shall deem reasonable. For the other services in criminal proceedings and in proceedings for the violation of any Ordinances or provisions of the Charter of the City of East Saginaw, such sums as the Common Council shall allow. For any persons committed to the City Jail by any Police Justice, twenty-five cents; for every person legally discharged from the City Jail, twenty cents.

SEC. 4. All claims for services by any Police Justice; City Marshal or City Constable, shall be in the form of a bill, showing specially the several items, and shall be accompanied by an affidavit that such service has been actually performed, and that the charges for the same are in accordance with this Ordinance, or that the services have been actually rendered, and that the charges therefor are reasonable as the case may be, and the accounts of

Claims to be in a form of a bill and accompanied by an affidavit.

the Marshal or City Constable under this Ordinance shall in addition have the certificate of a Police Justice of the City of East Saginaw, that the services therein mentioned have been actually performed.

To prohibit receiving illegal fees.

SEC. 5. No Officer or Magistrate in this Ordinance mentioned, shall receive any other or greater fee or reward for the services herein specified than is allowed by this Ordinance.

Service to be actually performed before demanding or receiving fees.

SEC. 6. No fee or compensation allowed by this Ordinance shall be demanded or received by any officer or person for any service, unless such service was actually rendered by him, but this section shall not be construed to prevent any officer from demanding and receiving from parties liable to pay the same, any fee herein allowed for any services of which he is entitled by law, to require the payment of, previous to rendering such service.

Penalty.

SEC. 7. For a violation of either of the said last sections, the person guilty on conviction thereof by a court having jurisdiction of the offence, shall pay a penalty of not exceeding ten dollars, or on being convicted, as aforesaid, and on failure to pay the said penalty, shall be confined in the City or County Jail not exceeding twenty days.

TITLE II.

OF SIDEWALKS, CROSSWALKS, &c.

CHAPTER XVII.

CONSTRUCTING AND REPAIRING SIDEWALKS AND CROSSWALKS.

[Ordinance Approved July 11th, 1859.]

Side and crosswalks to be paved or planked as the Common Council may direct.

SECTION 1. That the side and crosswalks of all streets which are or shall be graded, shall be paved or planked with such materials as the Common Council may direct.

How lots or premises are exempt.

SEC. 2. If the owner of any lot or premise has or shall have paved or planked the walk in front of his premises according to the provisions of this ordinance, and shall keep the same in good repair, such premises shall be exempt and the owner thereof shall not be liable to pay any assessment for sidewalks, upon his producing satisfactory evidence to the Marshal that such person has or shall have so paved or planked such sidewalk or paid therefor, and shall have kept the same in good repair, and no such exemption shall be allowed to any person or persons except in the manner and on the terms and conditions above expressed.

Owners authorized to pave or plank under the direction of the Marshal.

SEC. 3. The owners of all lots on streets which have been graded or prepared for the laying down of sidewalks under the direction of the Common Council, are hereby authorized to pave or plank in front of their lots under the direction of the Marshal as the Common Council may direct.

Assessments how made.

SEC. 4. Whenever the Common Council of said City shall deem it necessary to provide funds for defraying the expenses of paving and planking any sidewalks within the limits of said City, they shall do so by assessment on the owner or occupant of the lots or premises in front or adjacent to the sidewalks paved or planked or directed so to be, and whenever it may be necessary to provide for the expense of constructing any crosswalks in said City, the assessments for the same shall be made in accordance with the provisions of this ordinance particularly relating thereto.

Assessment to be made.

SEC. 5. Whenever the said Common Council shall have paved or planked any sidewalk in said City, or shall direct the same to be paved or planked; the Marshal or such other officer as may be appointed by the Common Council, shall make an assessment on the owner or occupant of the lots or premises in front of or adjacent to said sidewalks paved or planked, or directed so to be

Conditions of the Assessment roll

SEC. 6. The Marshal, or such other officer as may be appointed as aforesaid, shall with all due diligence ascertain from the best evidence in his power, all the necessary facts, and shall then make out a written report or assessment roll, stating therein the names of the owners or occupants of the lots or premises in front or adjacent to which such sidewalks may be paved or planked, or directed so to be, describing by itself with sufficient accuracy each lot or portion of a lot owned by any one person or company of persons, and also the names of such owner or several owners or occupants or either of them, he shall state such fact in his report, and he shall therein state who of such owners are residents of said City, and who are non-residents. The Marshal or such other officer as may be appointed, as aforesaid, shall also, in as accurate manner as possible, ascertain and in said report set forth the space or number of square yards or feet paved or planked, and the sum of money which such person or set of persons shall be assessed at and pay for such paving or planking and also five cents for each description to defray the expense of making such assessment, which report the Marshal or such other officer as may be appointed as aforesaid, shall present to said Common Council.

City Clerk to notify persons to be assessed.

SEC. 7. The Clerk shall then make out a notice directed to the several persons in said report named and proposed to be assessed, notifying them that they are about to be assessed, to defray the expenses of paving or planking the sidewalks adjacent to certain premises owned or occupied by them in said City, and that a report or assessment roll made out in the premises is on file in the office of said Clerk, for inspection and further notifying them of the time and place when the Common Council will meet and revise said report or assessment. On the request of any person conceiving himself aggrieved, which said notice shall be published in some newspaper printed in said City for two successive weeks.

SEC. 8 In addition to the notice, provided for in the last preceeding section, the Marshal, or such other officer as may be appointed, as aforesaid, as soon as any such assessment shall have been made, shall forthwith serve or cause to be served upon all persons therein interested, who are residents of the City, a written or printed notice by delivering the same personally, or leaving it at the parties usual place of abode or business, which said notice shall fully set forth the place where said sidewalk, paving or planking is ordered, and the said party is allowed ten days within which to construct the same, and, if completed within that time to the satisfaction of the Marshal, that no expense of proceeding to collect the same shall be incurred by them, and, upon the expiration of the said ten days, the Marshal or such other officer, as may be appointed, as aforesaid, shall make a full return to the Common Council of his doings, under this section, and state fully whether such notices have not been complied with by said parties. And if from such return it appears that such sidewalks, paving or planking have not been constructed within the ten days prescribed, by the parties notified, then the amount of such assessment together with the costs and charges incident to the collection thereof shall be collected by warrant under the hand of the Mayor, directed to the Marshal, commanding him to collect the amount of such assessment from the person or persons liable therefor and the Marshal shall thereupon proceed and levy the amount of such assessment and the costs and charges thereon, adding thereto four per cent. for his fees of the goods and chattels of said person or persons, if any such can be found in the County of Saginaw, and in case no such goods and chattles can be found, the amount shall be a lien on the premises on which the same was assessed, and shall be returned to the office of the Mayor, and shall be collected by sale of said premises in such manner as may be provided by the Charter and Ordinance of the City.

SEC. 9. The Common Council shall at the time and place in said section specified, or at some session thereafter, take said assessment into consideration, and if no person appears to object to said report or roll and no good cause appears to the contrary, and an affidavit of publication of the requisite notice having been made by some one acquainted with the facts, they shall, by a written resolution to be entered on their journal, declare that they approve of said report or assessment roll; that they receive as correct the descriptions of the premises and the names of the individuals therein contained, and that the same of which said report states to be the correct one which each individual or set of individuals should be assessed at, and pay, be the assessment, and be collected from the respective persons liable according to law. But if any sufficient cause appears, or it is shown to said Common Council, they shall review such report or roll and make such an assessment as may be just and right in the premises, and said Common Council may, if necessary, adjourn from one time to any reasonable time, for the purpose of finishing said review of said assessment.

SEC. 10. The Common Council may from time to time authorize that good and substantial sidewalks shall be laid down or constructed in any street, or part of a street, whether graded or not, as herein before described and under the direction of the Marshal or other officer.

Construction of sidewalks, etc.

SEC. 11. Such sidewalks shall be constructed of good pine plank, which shall not be less than two inches in thickness nor more than twelve inches wide, on oak, cedar or hemlock sleepers, not less than four inches square, to be placed not more than three feet apart, the plank to be nailed with nails not less than forty penny, with at least three in each end of each plank and not less than two at any other bearing, and said sidewalks shall be of the following width, viz: On Washington street from Potter street to the South City line, and on Genesee street, from Water street, to Hoyt street, and on Jefferson street from Genesee to

Hoyt street, at least eight feet wide and on the residue of said Washington, Genesee and Jefferson streets at least six feet; on all other streets, five feet: *Provided, however*, that the Common Council may at any time direct that such sidewalks or any part thereof to be of more or less width then is herein before described and all crosswalks shall be constructed of pine plank, not less than three inches thick and twelve inches wide; to be laid and fastened as in this section above described for sidewalks, such crosswalks to be of such width as shall be ordered by the Common Council; (*As amended by an Ordinance approved July* 1, 1867).

SEC. 12. When the Common Council shall direct the construction of any such plank sidewalk, the Marshal or such other officer as may be appointed shall proceed and make an assessment therefor, showing the names of the owners or occupants (residents or non-residents) of the premises in front of which such sidewalk is required, with the description of such premises, the length and width of such walk, and the sum of money to be assessed for constructing the same, and when such assessments shall be made.

SEC. 13. Whenever an assessment has been duly levied according to the provisions of this ordinance, and a return of the warrant issued for the collection of the same by the Marshal, under the provisions of section 8, has been made, the Common Council shall proceed to the construction of the sidewalks as ordered, and the property of all persons whose assessments have not been paid, shall be held liable for all costs, charges and interest incurred in their behalf in the construction of said sidewalks, and may be sold for the same as in the case of delinquent taxes.

SEC. 14. Whenever, by mistake or otherwise, any person may be improperly designated as the owner of any lot or premises in proceedings under ordinance or any of the ordinances of said City relative to taxes, or assessments, the tax or assessment shall not for such cause be vitiated, but the same shall be a lien on such lot or premise and be collected as in other cases.

SEC. 15. All crosswalks over the streets and alleys of this City shall be constructed under the direction of the Marshal and shall be paid for out of the General fund.

SEC. 16. Whenever any sidewalk, within the limits of said City, shall need re-building or repairing, the owners or occupants of lots or premises in front or adjacent to such sidewalk, shall be notified to rebuild or repair the same within such time as the Common Council may by resolution order and direct, and if said sidewalk shall not be rebuilt or repaired in compliance with such order of the Common Council, the Marshal shall cause the same to be rebuilt or repaired, and the same proceeding shall be adopted to assess and collect the expense thereof, as is required by this Ordinance for assessing and collecting the expense of building sidewalks: *Provided*, that the expense for rebuilding or repairing such sidewalk, shall exceed two dollars, to be assessed to the owner or occupannt as aforesaid, at any time.

This Section approved by Ordinance bearing date May 20, 1861.

CHAPTER XVIII.

SIDEWALKS AND CROSSWALKS.

[Ordinance Approved April 26th, 1868.]

Leading or driving animals upon sidewalks, prohibited. Penalty.

SECTION 1. No person shall drive or lead any swine, horse, sheep, goat or cattle upon or along and lengthwise thereupon any sidewalk in the City of East Saginaw, under a penalty of not exceeding five dollars for each and every offence.

Sidewalks not to be obstructed, etc. Penalty.

SEC. 2. No person shall place or deposit on any sidewalk, or in any street, any box, crate, cask, goods, wares or any merchandise under a penalty of two dollars for each offence, and the person placing or depositing the same, and the owner or occupant of the premises in front of which the same shall be, shall forfeit the further penalty for each and every two hours the same shall remain after they shall have been notified by the Mayor, an Alderman, Marshal or Deputy Marshal, to remove the same: *Provided*, that any person may place and leave for a period not exceeding four hours on four feet of the outer edge of the sidewalk in front of his store or building, any goods, wares or merchandise which he shall be in the act of receiving or delivering and any person to entitle him to the benefit of this proviso to this section, shall show by evidence, that his case is within such proviso.

SEC 3. No person shall push, lead, ride, draw, back or drive any horse, oxen, cart, wagon, sleigh or other vehicle over or upon any sidewalk, unless it be in crossing the same to go into a yard, stable or lot, nor place or leave any horse, oxen, waggon, cart, sleigh, fire engine, hose cart, or other vehicle on any crosswalk or sidewalk under the penalty of not less than one nor more than ten dollars for each and every offence.

No horse, etc., to be used on sidewalks.

CHAPTER XIX.

OF THE USE OF STREETS AND ALLEYS.

[Ordinance Approved October 24th, 1870.]

SECTION 1. No person shall permit any snow or ice to remain on the sidewalk in front of any house, building or lot, occupied by him or her, longer than twenty-four hours after the same has fallen or formed, and when ice is formed on any sidewalk, such owner or occupant as above provided shall within twelve hours after the same has formed, cause salt, ashes or sand to be strewn thereon.

Snow and Ice to be removed from sidewalks.

SEC. 2. No person shall remove or cause to be removed, or aid or assist in removing any building into, along or across any street, alley or other public space, without permission first obtained from the Mayor or Common Council.

Buildings not to be removed in streets without permission.

SEC. 3. No person shall run or propel any velocipede, truck or hand-cart, nor drive, lead or back any horse, mule, ox, cow or other animal or team, cart or wheel carriage, sleigh or other vehicle on any sidewalk.

Animals, etc., not to be driven on sidewalks.

SEC. 4. No person owning building or repairing any house or other building, shall permit any lumber, brick, plaster, mortar, earth, clay, sand, stone or other material to remain on the sidewalk after sunset of the day upon which it was placed there without the permission of the Mayor or Common Council.

Building material not to remain on sidewalks.

SEC. 5. No person shall obstruct or encumber any public wharf, sidewalk, street, alley or other public space with any article or thing whatever. This section shall not be construed to prohibit merchants and other business persons from using and occupying the side of the sidewalks next to their place of business for a

Streets, wharfs, etc. not to be obstructed.

distance of three feet, for the purpose of displaying their goods, wares or merchandise, nor shall it be so construed as to prevent the moving of goods, wares or merchandise across any sidewalk in the way of trade, or for the use of families. No person shall erect or maintain any sign or show-case which shall extend more than three feet from the building into or over any street or sidewalk.

Vehicles not to stand in streets.

SEC. 6. No person shall leave any carriage, cart, wagon, sleigh or other vehicle standing in any street, alley or public space, without the same is actually in use at the time.

Building materials not to be placed in streets without permission.

SEC. 7. No person shall place by himself or any other, any stone, timber, lumber, plank, boards, brick or other materials in or upon any street, alley or other public space, except for the purpose of building, and not for that purpose except under the permission first obtained from the Mayor or Common Council, and such materials shall not be allowed to remain in such street, alley or other public space after the completion of said building, or for a longer period than four months, and the same shall not be allowed to occupy and obstruct more than one-half of any street or alley, and after such building has been completed, all building material, dirt and rubbish arising therefrom shall be removed.

Animals to be tied, etc.

SEC. 8. No person shall leave any horse, mule, oxen or team in any street, alley or public space without being sufficiently tied, and no person shall halt any wagon, cart, carriage, sleigh or other vehicle on any cross-walk.

Construct'n of drains and sewers.

SEC. 9. No person shall make or construct any drain in any street or other public space, within four feet of the curbstone of the sidewalk, unless it be a drain or sewer leading to and from the building or lot from which the same is designed.

Digging up and replacing pavements.

SEC. 10. No person shall dig or tear up any pavement, side or crosswalk, or dig any hole, ditch, drain or sewer in any street, alley or other public space without permission first obtained from the Mayor, Common Council or Street Commissioner, and it shall be the duty of any person digging any hole, ditch, drain or sewer in any street, alley or other public space, as speedily as practicably, to repair and put the same in as good order and condition as before, and in order to do this, such person shall pound down the earth so as to make it firm and solid, and if the earth shall settle, such person shall fill the same from time to time as may be necessary, and any person digging in any street, alley or public space, for any of the purposes herein before mentioned or for any purpose whatever, shall erect and maintain a good and sufficient fence, railing or barrier around such excavation in such a manner as to prevent accidents and to place and keep upon such railing, fence or barrier, suitable and sufficient colored lights during the night.

SEC. 11. It shall be the duty of every owner or occupant of any house or building in said City at all times to keep the drains or gutter in front of or adjacent to the lot on which such building is situated, clear and free from any obstructions that may hinder the free passage of water therein.

Drains and gutters to be kept free and clear.

SEC. 12. No person shall cart or throw or cause to be thrown into any drain, sewer or gutter within said City, any straw, shavings, wood, stones, brick, rubbish or any filth or other substance or cause any obstruction, nuisance or injury in or to the same by diverting or stopping the water course thereof or otherwise.

Straw, etc., not to be thrown in drains, gutters or sewers.

SEC. 13. It shall not be lawful for any carpenter, stone mason or any other peason, to use or occupy any street, lane or alley in said City for the purpose of framing timber or cutting, sawing or chopping stone, unless by permission of the Common Council.

Stone masons, etc. not to obstruct streets without permission.

SEC. 14. No person shall herd together or detain in any street, alley or other public space, any cattle, horses, hogs, sheep or goats.

Cattle not to be herded in streets.

SEC. 15. No person shall place or put any trough for feeding or watering horses, cattle or animals in any street, alley or other public space.

Cattle troughs.

SEC. 16. No person shall keep or maintain on any sidewalk any wagon or stand for the sale of goods, wares or merchandise, vegetables or fruits to project more than three feet from the wall of his or her house or store.

Stands on sidewalks.

SEC. 17. No person shall display any stud horse in any street, alley or public space.

Exhibition of stud horses prohibited.

SEC. 18. No person shall ride or drive any horse, carriage, sleigh or other vehicle through any street or avenue in this City at a faster rate than six miles per hour.

Fast driving through the streets prohibited.

Balustrade and balconies.

SEC. 19. No person shall erect any balustrade or balcony, to extend beyond the line of any street and less than twelve feet from the ground, without permission first obtained from the Common Council, and iron braces and railings shall be used in the construction of any such balustrade or balconies, and the same shall not project beyond the line of the street more than three feet.

Games not be played on streets.

SEC. 20. No person shall play any game of nine or ten pins, ball wicket or other games in any street, alley or other public space.

No crowds gathered.

SEC. 21. It shall not be lawful to gather in crowds on any sidewalk or in any street, so as to obstruct travel therein or encumber the same.

Hitching posts.

SEC. 22. No post, except for the purpose of supporting awnings or hitching horses shall be erected, put up or maintained in any street, alley or public space without permission first obtained from the Common Council.

Awning posts.

SEC. 23. No wooden post for the purpose of supporting any awning shall be erected or set up in any paved street, avenue or public space, and all iron posts erected in any paved street, avenue or other public space for the purpose of supporting awnings, shall not be less than eight feet in height and to be placed next to and along side of the curbstone, and no rails or strips of boards shall be used to connect such posts with the buildings.

Awnings.

SEC. 24. No awning or cloth canvass used as an awning shall be permitted to hang within six and one-half feet of the sidewalk.

Suspended lamps, signs, goods, etc.

SEC. 25. No person shall suspend from any house, shop, awning or otherwise, into or over any street, alley or other public space, any lamp, sign, goods, clothes, wares or other articles or substances so that the same shall extend or project from the wall or front of such building more than three feet.

Cellar doors, etc.

SEC. 26. No person shall make or contiuue any cellar door, windows or area, so that the same shall extend more than five feet beyond the line of any street, and all areas shall be protected by sufficient grating or illuminated pavement.

SEC. 27. Every entrance or flight of steps projecting beyond the line of the street, or descending into any cellar or basement story, where such entrance or flight of steps shall not be covered, shall be enclosed in a good iron railing on each side, permanently put up, not less than two feet nine inches high with a gate opening inwardly unless such entrance steps be thoroughly lighted so as to prevent accidents; and such steps and railing shall not occupy more than one-fifth of the width of the sidewalk. Entrances.

SEC. 28. No person shall construct or continue any porch over a cellar door so that the same shall project beyond the line of any alley or other public space. Porches.

SEC. 29. No person shall dig or construct or cause to be dug or constructed any area to or around any cellar or basement story so that the same shall extend more than four feet beyond the line of any street, and no vault shall be dug or constructed to extend beyond the curb line of the street. Areas.

SEC. 30. No person shall swim or bathe in any of the waters in or adjoining the City of East Saginaw, so as to be exposed to the view of spectators. Bathing in sight of spectators prohibited.

SEC. 31. No person shall place, or allow to be placed, or remain in any window of any building, or room of said building in said City, which he or she may occupy, which is built along the the line of any street or alley, any earthern pot, vessel or other substance whatever, which would endanger the safety of any person passing along said street or alley, if the same should fall from said window, without the same is inside, a sufficient rack or band to prevent the same from falling from said window into the street or alley below. Earthen pots, etc., not to be placed in windows.

SEC. 32. No person shall hoist or raise from any street into any building, loft, store or room, or lower from any building, store, loft or room into any street, any cask, bale, bundle, box, crate or any goods, wares or merchandise, boards, joists, timber or article whatever, by means of any rope, pulley, tackle or windlass. Hoisting goods, etc.

SEC. 33. When any street or lane is crowded with teams, wagons or other vehicles, or through which any civic, military or funeral procession is passing, every person having charge of any Crowded teams, etc. Civic or funeral processions, etc.

horse, team, wagon or other vehicle shall obey any order for the removal of such horse, team, wagon or other vehicle given by the Mayor, Alderman, Marshal, or any Policeman.

No building removed on street without consent.

SEC. 34. No person shall remove, or cause to be removed, any building through any street in the City of East Saginaw, without the written permission of the Mayor or vote of the Common Council.

No building to be moved on planked or paved streets.

SEC. 35. No person shall remove or cause to be removed, any building upon the planked or paved portions of Water, Washington, Genesee or Hoyt streets, or the planked or paved portion of any other street. In case of necessity, the Common Council may grant permission to remove buildings across said street, and to remove buildings standing upon said streets.

No building to stand over three days on any street.

SEC. 36. No person removing any building shall suffer or permit the same to stand on any street, lane, alley or public ground for a longer period than three days.

No omnibus to pass another when moving four miles per hour.

SEC. 37. No driver of any omnibus shall pass or attempt to pass any other omnibus while the same is moving at the rate of four miles per hour.

Teams not to be left on the streets unhitched.

SEC. 38. No person shall leave any horse or horses, whether attached or unattached, to any carriage, wagon, cab or other vehicle standing on any street, lane, alley or public ground, unless the same be securely fastened, or the reins be in his or her hands, or within his or her reach, or in the hands, or within the reach of some person competent to manage or control the same.

Funeral procession not to be interrupted.

SEC. 39. No person shall drive any horse or carriage, or vehicle of any kind, through any funeral procession.

Sliding or skating on streets or sidewalks prohibited.

SEC. 40. No person shall slide or coast upon hand sleds or skates in any street or sidewalk in said City.

Certain streets not to be occupied for sale of wood.

SEC. 41. No person or persons shall be permitted to occupy any portion of Genesee street, west of the east line of Jefferson street, for the sale of wood or hay.

Penalty.

SEC. 42. Any violation of the provisions of this ordinance shall be punished by a fine not to exceed one hundred dollars and costs of prosecution, and in the imposition of any such fine and costs, the court may make a further sentence, that in default of the payment thereof, such offender be imprisoned in the City prison or County jail for a period of time not exceeding thirty days.

SEC. 43. It is hereby made the duty of the Marshal, Assistant Marshal, Policeman and Street Commissioner of the City, to see that the provisions of this ordinance are faithfully observed, and to make complaint for all violation of the same. Marshal, etc to enforce ordinance.

SEC. 44. An ordinance entitled "An Ordinance relative to the use of streets and alleys," made and passed the 11th day of July, A. D. 1859, be and the same is hereby repealed. Repealed.

CHAPTER XX.

LAMPS AND LAMP POSTS.

[Ordinance Approved December 21st, 1868.]

SECTION 1. The public lamps and lamp posts of the City of East Saginaw shall be under the control of the Mayor, Marshal and the Standing Committee of the Common Council on Gas, who shall see that the same is properly set as ordered by the Common Council, that they are kept in proper repair, and that all regulations and ordinances of the Common Council relative to to lighting, cleaning, protecting and repairing the same are carried into effect. Under control of Mayor etc.

SEC. 2. No person shall wilfully maliciously or negligently injure, break, pull down, remove or in any manner deface any public lamp, lamp-post, crotchet or gas light, or incite any other person, or in any way cause the same to be done, within the limits of the City of East Saginaw. Lamp and lamp posts not to be injured.

SEC. 3. No person shall light or cause to be lighted or extinguished or caused to be extinguished any public lamp or gas light, without being authorized so to do by the Mayor, Marshal, Committee on Gas, or the East Saginaw Gas Light Company, or by resolution of the Common Council Nor lighted, nor extinguished without authority.

SEC. 4. No person shall hang or place any article or substance whatever upon or place any box, lumber, timber or other heavy material, against, or hitch any team, horse or any animal whatever to any public lamp or lamp post within said City. Animals not be hitched to lamp posts.

SEC. 5. No person shall erect, place or suspend any gas lamp or lamp post in any public street, park, square, lane, alley or place in said City, without permission from the Common Council. Lamps not to be suspended or lamp posts erected without authority.

Penalty.

SEC. 6. Any violation of the provisions of this ordinance shall be punished by a fine not less than five dollars and costs, nor to exceed the sum of fifty dollars and costs, for each offence upon conviction had before the Cecorder's court or any Justice of the Peace in and for said City, and in the imposition of said fine and costs, the court may make a further sentence, that the offender be imprisoned until the payment thereof not exceeding ninety days.

Duty of Marshal and Policemen.

SEC. 7. It is the especial duty of the Marshal and Police of said City to report any injury to said lamps and lamp posts to the Mayor without delay, and to make summary arrests and prosecute for all violations of this ordinance.

CHAPTER XXI.

OF THE PREVENTION OF ACCIDENTS.

[Ordinance Approved July 11th, 1870.]

Barriers to be erected.

SECTION 1. It shall be the duty of each and every person engaged in paving any avenue, street, lane or alley, or in digging or building any sewer, drain, trench or cistern in or through any avenue, street, lane or alley, or in the performance of any work whatever requiring the digging or excavating of any street, avenue, lane or alley, under a contract with the City of East Saginaw, or by virtue of any permission granted by the Common Council, or any department or officer of the City, when, if left exposed, such work would be dangerous to passengers; to erect and maintain a good and sufficient fence, railing or barrier around the same in such a manner as to prevent accidents; and it shall also be the duty of such person to place upon such railing, fence or barrier, at twilight on each day, suitable and sufficient colored lights, and keep them burning during the night.

Contracts for public work must contain provisions for erecting barriers, etc.

SEC. 2. It shall be the duty of the City Attorney or other legal adviser to insert in all contracts for paving or grading streets, avenues, lanes or alleys, or for constructing sewers, drains or reservoirs, or for doing any work whatever whereby accidents or injuries may occur in consequence of any neglect or carelessness on the part of the contractor, a covenant, requiring the contractor to place and maintain the fences, railing or barriers, in the manner provided for in the preceding section for the prevention of accidents, and keep and save the City harmless and indemnified against all loss and damage which may be occasioned by reason of any negligence or carelessness in the manner of doing such work.

SEC. 3. In all cases when any person or persons shall perform any work as provided in the preceding section, either under contract with the corporation or by virtue of any permission from the Common Council, or any department or officer of the City, such person shall be liable to the City of East Saginaw for any and every loss or damage which said corporation may sustain, and for all sums which it may have to pay to any person or persons by reason of any loss or injury sustained in consequence of any carelessness or negligence in doing the work, or by reason of any neglect or failure to comply with the provisions of this ordinance. Liability of contractors.

SEC. 4. Any person performing work as provided in this Ordinance, who shall neglect or refuse to comply with its provisions, shall be punished by a fine not to exceed one hundred dollars and costs, and in the imposition of any such fine or costs, the court may make a further sentence that the offender may be imprisoned in the city prison or county jail until the payment thereof, for a period of time not exceeding thirty days. Penalty.

TITLE III.

OF THE NAVIGATION OF SAGINAW RIVER.

CHAPTER XXII.

OF HARBOR MASTERS.

[Ordinance Approved July 11th, 1870.]

Vessels, etc., not to approach within 50 feet of docks.

SECTION 1. No steam tug or other vessel, while having one or more vessels in tow, and no vessel while made fast to any other vessel, by lines or otherwise, shall approach within fifty feet of any dock in said City, unless compelled to do so by unavoidable accident: *Provided*, this section shall not be so construed as to prevent steam tugs from approaching other vessels to take them in tow.

Navigation not to be impeded.

SEC. 2. No person shall throw or deposit in said river, within the City limits, any substances which may in any respect tend to injure the navigation thereof.

Vessels to maintain lights.

SEC. 3. All steamboats, ships, brigs or other vessels shall have kept on board during the night time a conspicuous light, elevated at least six feet above decks.

To move slowly.

SEC. 4. All steamboats, coming to or going from the docks, shall be moved under a low head of steam and slowly, so as not to endanger the docks and other crafts in port.

No vessel to be moored to bridge.

SEC. 5. No steamboat, vessel, tug, barge or lighter shall be run into, obstruct, or be moored or tied to any bridge in said City, or in any way use the same, except to pass the regular and proper draw therein in the usual and lawful manner.

SEC. 6. No raft of logs, lumber or timber shall be hitched, moored or fastened to, or left at any dock in said City, without the consent of the owner of such dock shall be first obtained therefor. No raft of logs, etc., to be moored at dock without consent of owners.

SEC. 7. No person shall unload any boat or vessel at or on any of the public wharves or dock in said City, or otherwise place or deposit on any such wharf or dock any stone, lumber, timber or firewood, or other material, without permission from the Harbor Master. Vessels unloading to obtain permission.

SEC. 8. The Common Council may annually appoint, at their third annual meeting, in the month of April or as soon thereafter as may be, a Harbor Master for the port of East Saginaw, who shall hold office for one year, subject to removal under the charter—the person first appointed under this Ordinance to hold until the third Monday in April, 1871. Before entering upon his office he shall give a bond to the said City, with sufficient sureties, conditioned to faithfully discharge the duties of this office, and perform the duties required of him by this Ordinance—in the penal sum of one thousand dollars—and in case of the sickness, or other disability of said Harbor Master, he may appoint a deputy, subject to the approval of the Common Council, to perform his duties during such sickness or disability. Harbor master appoint'd and term of office.

SEC. 9 Such Harbor Master, when appointed as herein provided for, shall receive such salary as the Council may fix, which shall be paid monthly: *Provided*, no salary shall be paid in any one year for such services, before the first day of April, and shall cease on the first day of December in each year. Salary.

SEC. 10. It shall be the duty of said Harbor Master to enforce the execution of the several provisions of this ordinance and of all other laws and ordinances passed by the Common Council for regulating and preserving the navigation of said Saginaw River within the limits of said City, and to make the necessary complaint for the violation thereof. Duties.

SEC. 11. The Harbor Master authorized to be appointed by this ordinance shall have authority to protect the owners and occupants of wharves and docks within the limits of the City, in the free and undisturbed use of the same. And he is authorized to regulate the anchorage of all vessels lying within said City limits, Powers.

and to give such order and directions relative to the location and change of station of every steamboat or other vessel, as shall be for the interest of trade and navigation, having respect, at all times, to the rights of occupants of wharves and docks; and to this end he shall have full authority to go on board of and move any steamboat or vessel that shall be without right or consent occupying any of said docks and wharves; and every owner, captain, master, consignee or other person, having in charge any such steamboat or vessel, shall be liable to the penalty of this ordinance for refusing to comply with such order or direction.

Penalty.

SEC. 12. Every owner, master, captain, consignee or any other person having in charge any steamboat or other vessel, used in violation of this ordinance, and any person or persons violating or failing to comply with the provisions thereof, shall be punished by a fine not exceeding one hundred dollars and costs of prosecution, and in the imposition of such fine and costs, the court may make a further sentence that the offenders be imprisoned in the City prison or county jail, until payment thereof, for a term not exceeding thirty days.

Harbor master to have power of special Policeman.

SEC. 13. The Harbor Master appointed under and by virtue of this ordinance, is hereby invested with all the powers of Special Policeman, appointed without pay from the City.

SEC. 14. "An Ordinance to establish the powers and duties of Harbor Master," made and passed by the Common Council, July 11th, 1859, is hereby repealed.

CHAPTER XXIII.

OF UNLOADING WATER CRAFTS ON SUNDAY.

[Ordinance Approved May 16th, 1870.]

No person shall load or unload water craft on Sunday.

SECTION 1. That no person shall load or unload, or assist to load or unload, any water craft on the Saginaw River within the limits of this City, on the first day of the week called Sunday: *Provided, however,* that nothing in this ordinance shall be so construed as to prevent the unloading of perishable property, which would otherwise be destroyed by remaining on board of said water craft.

SEC. 2. Any person who shall violate the provisions of this ordinance shall be punishable by a fine not exceeding one hundred dollars and costs of prosecution, and in the imposition of any such fine and cost, the court may make a further sentence that in default of the payment thereof, such offender be imprisoned in the county jail of Saginaw county, or the City prison, for a period of time not exceeding thirty days. Penalty.

CHAPTER XXIV.

OF LINE OF DOCKS.

[Ordinance Approved Feb. 23, 1863.]

SECTION 1. The line of docks on Saginaw River in this City shall be established as follows: Commencing at a point two hundred and thirty and three-tenth feet westerly from the intersection of the north line of Whitney street, with the west line of Water street, measuring on line running at an angle of eighty-three (83) degrees and thirty (30) minutes with the west line of Water street, thence to a point one hundred and sixty-four (164) feet distant from the center of Water and Miller street, westerly and at right angles with water street, thence on a line to a point two hundred feet westerly and at right angles with Water street from the center of Thompson and Water streets, thence on a line to a point one hundred and forty-eight (148) feet westerly and at right angles with Water street, from the center of McCroskey and Water streets, thence on a line to a point one hundred and thirty-four (134) feet westerly and at right angles with Water street from the center of Bristol and Water streets [*Amended March* 15, 1869.] To establish a line of docks. Boundaries of the line of docks.

SEC. 2. No person or persons owning or in possession of Water lot or lots within the line designated in the preceding section, shall hereafter build any dock thereon extending beyond the western boundary of said line mentioned in section one. To prohibit building docks beyond the Western boundary.

SEC. 3. All persons owning docks within said limits, extending beyond or west of the line described in section one of this ordin- To conform to said line of docks.

Penalty.

ance, shall cause the same to conform to said line within six months from this date, and for each day any such person shall refuse or neglect to comply with this section, he shall be liable to pay a fine for the use of this City, of not more than ten dollars, nor less than five dollars, to be imposed and collected in the manner prescribed in the following section.

Penalty for violating Sec. 2 and 3 of this Ordinance.

SEC. 4. Any person or persons violating section two of this ordinance, shall, on conviction thereof, foreit and pay a fine for the use of this City, not exceeding one hundred dollars, nor less than fifty dollars for each offence, to be prosecuted for and recovered in behalf of said City, and in case of each conviction under section two or three hereof, the Common Council may by resolution, order or direct any dock being within said limits contrary to said sections, to be removed: *Provided*, the owner, agent or occupant of such dock be previously notified by said Council to remove such dock, or such portion thereof as may extend into the river beyond said boundary line, and, in case of neglect or refusal by the owner, agent or occupant to remove the same within sixty days as provided for in the following section, the Common Council shall have power to remove the same, and the expense thereof, which may be sued for and recovered in the name of said City, in any court of competent jurisdiction.

Publication and service of resolution

SEC. 5. A notice and copy of the resolution mentioned in the last preceeding section, shall be published at least one week in some newspaper printed and circulated in said City, and a certified copy of such resolution shall be personally served upon the owner, agent or occupant of such dock, if residing in this City, at least ten days previous to the removal of such dock by the order of the Common Council.

TITLE IV.

OF SALES.

CHAPTER XXV.

OF HAWKERS AND PEDDLERS.

[Ordinance Approved May 20th, 1867.]

SECTION 1. Each and every person or persons owning or having in his or their possession any goods, wares or merchandise, brought into said City, to be disposed of at public auction or vendue, shall before exposing any such goods, wares or merchandise for sale as aforesaid, except in case of sales authorized by law apply to and obtain from the City Clerk a license therefor, and before receiving said license shall pay to the said clerk for the use of said City the duties hereinafter prescribed. Auctioneers to obtain license.

SEC. 2. It shall be the duty of the City Clerk to issue licenses for the sale of goods, wares and merchandise at public auction or vendue, as follows: For the period of not more than thirty days upon the payment to him of the sum of twenty dollars which license shall not be assignable; for the period of one year, upon the payment of the sum of fifty dollars, and every license shall express on its face the period for which it is granted. City Clerk to issue.

SEC. 3. Every person violating the provisions of this ordinance shall upon conviction thereof be punished by a fine not exceeding one hundred dollars, nor less than fifty dollars, and in default of the payment of such fine, shall be imprisoned in the City prison or County Jail of Saginaw County, for a term of not less than twenty days nor more than thirty days in the discretion of the court. Penalty.

CHAPTER XXVI.

OF TRANSIENT AUCTIONEERS.

[Ordinance Approved August 15th, 1870.]

Transient persons selling goods, etc., at auction to have license.

SECTION 1. That each and every transient person or persons owning or having in his or their possession any goods, wares or merchandise brought into said City to be disposed of at public auction or vendue of the value of five hundred dollars or more, shall, before exposing for sale any such goods, wares or merchandise aforesaid, except in case of sales authorized by law, apply to the Clerk of this City for a license therefor, and before receiving such license, shall pay to the City Treasurer, for the use of the City, the sum of twenty-five dollars per day for any day or part of a day he shall expose said goods, wares or merchandise at auction in said City.

The words goods, wares or merchandise in this section shall not be construed so as to include wood or fuel, or the products of the farm or dairy, when exposed or offered for sale by the producers thereof.

Penalty.

SEC. 2. Every person violating the provisions of this ordinance shall upon conviction thereof be punished by a fine not less than fifty dollars nor more than one hundred dollars for each offence, and in default of the payment of such fine shall be imprisoned in the City Prison or County Jail of Saginaw County for a term not less than twenty days nor more than thirty days in the discretion of the court.

Marshal, etc. to see Ordinances observed.

SEC. 3. The Marshal and his Assistants are instructed to see that this ordinance is observed.

Persons liable to carrying on business without license.

SEC. 4. That for each and every day or part of a day any such person or person shall carry on business without a license therefor as provided in section one, they shall be liable in addition to any fine imposed, to pay the sum of twenty-five dollars per day for any day or part of a day they may have done business without a license.

CHAPTER XXVII.

OF PEDDLING IN PUBLIC STREETS.

[Ordinance Approved August 2d, 1869.]

SECTION 1. No person shall by himself or by his servant, or agent expose for sale, nor sell in any of the public streets or grounds, in this City, from wagons, carts, carriages or other vehicle or vehicles, nor from stands, any patent medicines or other medicines or nostrums, or any other goods or merchandise whatever: *Provided*, this section shall not apply to sales by public officers by virtue of any legal process, nor to sales of household goods or merchandise by resident and properly licensed auctioneers. Nostrums, etc., not to be sold on street.

SEC. 2. Each person who shall violate the provisions of the preceding section of this ordinance, shall on conviction thereof, pay a fine of not less than five dollars nor more than one hundred dollars together with the costs of prosecution. Penalty.

CHAPTER XXVIII.

OF BELL RINGING.

[Ordinance Approved July 11th, 1859.]

SECTION 1. No bell shall be rung in or about the streets of this City, for the purpose of collecting bidders at any auction, nor shall any crier be employed for that purpose nor shall any bell be so rung or crier employed for any other purpose without a special permit from the Mayor or three members of the Council. Permit to ring bells, etc.

SEC. 2. Whoever shall violate any of the provisions of the foregoing sections, shall forfeit and pay not less than five nor more than fifty dollars for every offense, and the bell ringer or crier shall be deemed equally guilty with the person employing them. Penalty.

CHAPTER XXIX.

OF PAWN BROKERS.

[Ordinance Approved June 27th, 1870.]

Pawnbrokers must be licensed. SECTION 1. No person shall engage in the business of a Pawnbroker, in the City of East Saginaw, without having first obtained from the proper officers of the City, a license in proper form, as required by the City Charter, to do business as such Pawnbroker.

Condition of license and license fee. SEC. 2. The Clerk is hereby authorized to issue a license to any person of good character, to engage in the business of a Pawnbroker in the City of East Saginaw, on his paying into the City Treasury the sum of twenty-five dollars, and executing a bond to the corporate City of East Saginaw, in the penal sum of five hundred dollars with one or more sufficient sureties, to be approved by the Common Council, conditioned that he will faithfully observe the provisions of this ordinance.

Not more than one shop kept under one license. SEC. 3. No person licensed as a Pawnbroker under this ordinance, shall by virtue of one license, keep more than one house, shop or place for taking goods in pawn.

Pawnb'kers to keep signs. SEC. 4. Every person licensed under this ordinance, shall cause his name or the name of the firm with the words "Licensed Pawnbroker," to be painted in large, eligible character and placed over the outside of the door of his shop or place of business.

To keep books. SEC. 5. Every Pawnbroker shall keep a book in which shall be legibly written at the time of each loan, an accurate description of the goods, articles or things pawned, the date and time of pledging the same, the amount of money loaned thereon, the rate of interest to be paid on such loan, the time within which such pawn is to be redeemed, and the name and residence of the person pledging the said goods, articles or thing, and when a watch is pledged with any Pawnbroker, he shall also write in such book the number and name of the maker thereof, and when jewelry or gold or silver articles of any kind are pledged, he shall note in such book all letters or marks inscribed thereon; and whenever any goods, articles or things of any kind shall be sold at auction as hereinafter provided, the date of such sale, the amount for which the same was sold, and the name of the purchaser thereof shall also be entered in such book.

SEC. 6. Every Pawnbroker shall at the time of making any loan, and receiving any article in pledge therefore, deliver to the person from whom he received it, a memorandum in writing, signed by him, containing the date and amount of such loan, the rate of interest to be paid thereon, the time within which such article is to be redeemed, with a full description of the same, as provided in the preceeding section. To deliver receipt.

SEC. 7. The book provided for in section five in this ordinance shall at all times be open to the inspection of the Mayor and Chief of Police of the City of East Saginaw. Entry book to be open to Mayor and Chief of Police.

SEC. 8. No Pawnbroker shall sell any article or thing which may have been left with him in pledge, until the same shall have remained in his possession at least two months beyond the time in which the same was to have been redeemed, and the sale of the same shall be at public auction, after being advertised for at least ten days in at least one daily paper, published in said City, and such sale shall be conducted by a licensed auctioneer of the City of East Saginaw, and not otherwise. Pawnb'kers sale to be advertised.

SEC. 9. The surplus money, if any, arising from any sale, as provided in the preceeding section, after deducting the amount of the loan, interest and charges due on the same shall be paid over by such Pawnbroker to the person who would have been entitled to redeem such article, if no sale had taken place; and if the owner of such surplus money shall not call for the same within one month after such sale, the same shall be paid into the City treasury. Surplus of proceeds of sale to be returned to pledger.

SEC. 10. It shall be the duty of all Pawnbrokers licensed under this ordinance, on receiving information, that any article or thing left with them in pledge has been lost or stolen, to notify, in writing, the Chief of Police of the fact, giving the name of the person from whom they received the same, and time when it was received. To notify Chief of Police of lost or stolen article pledged.

SEC. 11. No Pawnbroker shall purchase any article or thing offered to him as a pledge. Not to purchase articles offered as pledge.

Not to receive pledges from infants or drunkards.

SEC. 12. No Pawnbroker shall receive in pledge any article or thing from any person under sixteen years of age, or who is intoxicated, or who is a habitual or common drunkard.

Nor from apprentices or servants.

SEC. 13. No Pawnbroker shall knowingly take from any apprentice or servant any article or thing offered by them in pledge, without first ascertaining that such article or thing is the property of the person so offering the same in pledge.

Penalty.

SEC. 14. Any violation of or failure to comply with the provisions of this ordinance, shall be punished by a fine not to exceed one hundred dollars and costs, and in the imposition of any fine and costs, the court may make a further sentence that the offender be imprisoned in the City prison or county jail until payment thereof; *Provided*, No person shall be sentenced or imprisoned for a period exceeding ninety days.

TITLE V.

OF THE PUBLIC HEALTH.

CHAPTER XXX.

OF THE BOARD OF HEALTH.

[Ordinance Approved May 21st, 1866.]

SECTION 1. The Chairman of the Committee of Health, the Street Commissioner, the City Marshal, the City Physician and one other physician to be designated by a vote of the Common Council, shall be and are hereby constituted a Board of Health in and for the City of East Saginaw, with the power and duties prescribed in the charter and this ordinance. To create a Board of Health.

SEC. 2. The Chairman of the Committee on Health shall be President of the "Board of Health" and preside at its meetings. President.

SEC. 3. The Board of Health may meet at the Common Council room or at any other more convenient place at such times as they shall deem proper. The City Clerk shall be the clerk of the Board of Health and shall keep regular minutes of their proceedings in books to be provided for that purpose. The City Attorney shall when required by the Board act as its legal adviser and draw any rules, regulations, resolutions or motions by the Board ordered or deemed necessary. Where the Board may meet. Clerk and City Attorney's duty.

SEC. 4. The Board of Health shall have power and it shall be their duty. Power and duties.

1. To do such acts and perform such duties and cause to be observed the provisions specified and given in title ten of the charter.

To make inquiry.

2. To make and direct to be made diligent inquiry with respect to all nuisances of any description within said City, which are or may be injurious to the public health and abate the same.

To inspect all places that may need cleaning.

3. To enter upon the premises and into any house, shop, manufactory or place or buildings of any kind or description in the City, as often as they or any of its members shall deem necessary or the Board shall order and examine into the health, cleanliness and number of persons occupying and inhabiting the same, and inspect the cellars, rooms, sinks, vaults, cisterns, privies, sewers, yards and premises, and make such orders, rules, directions, and regulations concerning the same or any of them as shall in the opinion of the Board of Health be proper or necessary for the cleaning, filling up, purifying, draining or keeping clean, pure and drained and for the health of the occupants, the neighbors or the City.

As to service of orders.

SEC. 5. All orders, regulations, directions and rules of the Board of Health shall be served on all persons, owners or occupants to be affected thereby, and if such person, owner or occupants to be affected thereby, shall not observe, keep and perform the same as to any and all cleaning, draining, filling up, purifying and regulating any house, building, yards, grounds, business shops, cellars, sewers, drains, barns, pens or other place or thing within said City, that shall be unwholesome, sunken, damp, foul, incumbered with filth, rubbish, or any other matter or thing that is or may become unwholesome, offensive or disagreeable. and for filling and amending all sinks, cellars, vaults and privies within said City, or for any work that may be necessary for the purposes aforesaid or for the preservation of the public health then the same shall be done at the expense of the City, under the direction of the Street Commissioner on account of the persons respectively upon whom the same may be assessed and for that purpose the expenses thereof shall be estimated, assessed and collected and the lands therewith sold in case of non-payment in the same manner as is provided by law with respect to other public improvements.

Penalty.

SEC. 6. Any violation of or failure to comply with the provisions of this ordinance, and any violation of or neglect to comply with any of the rules, regulations, orders or requirements of the Board of Health, shall on complaint be punished by a fine not to exceed one hundred dollars, and in the imposition of any such fine the court may make a further sentence that the offender on failure to pay such fine shall be imprisoned not exceeding ninety days.

CHAPTER XXXI.

OF THE PRESERVATION OF HEALTH, ETC.

[Ordinance Approved September 10th, 1866.]

SECTION 1. All low and sunken lots within the limits of the City of East Saginaw, shall be filled up even with the grade of the street or streets adjacent thereto, or to such depth as the Common Council shall direct, and with such material or materials and in such manner as the Common Council shall designate. *Low and sunken lots to be filled.*

SEC. 2. The owner or owners of such lots, as the Common Council shall direct to be filled up, are hereby authorized to fill the same, under the direction of the Street Commissioner and City Surveyor, with such material or materials, and in such manner and within such time as the Common Council shall designate. *Owners of such lots authorized to fill.*

SEC. 3. The Common Council may from time to time direct by an entry in the minutes, the lots and parts of lots to be filled, which entry shall contain a description of the lots and parts of lots, and specify the depth to which they are to be filled, the material or materials to be used and the time allowed the owner of said property to fill up the same. *Common Council may direct lots to be filled.*

SEC. 4. Whenever the Common Council shall direct any lots to be filled up, it shall be the duty of the Street Commissioner to ascertain the proper description and the names of the owners of the lots embraced in the order of the Common Council, and he shall forthwith serve or cause to be served upon all the persons, a written or partly written and partly printed notice, by delivering the same to them personally, or leaving at the parties' usual place of abode or business, or when the persons interested are non- *Duty of Street Commissioner in such cases.*

residents or cannot be found, by posting such notice in some conspicuous place on said lots, which notice shall fully set forth the descriptions of said lots, and the depth to which they are to be filled, and the material or materials to be used and the time allowed the owners to fill the same, and such [shall] also mail a copy of such notice to the owner at his post office address according to the best information he can obtain by inquiry in the City

Street Commissioner to make report and present to City Surveyor.

SEC. 5. If upon the expiration of the time prescribed for the filling of said lots, by the owner thereof, the said lots have not been filled up by the parties notified, the Street Commissioner shall with all due dilligence ascertain from the best evidence in his power all the necessary facts, and shall make out a written report or assessment roll, stating therein the names of the owners of said lots directed to be filled up, describing by itself with sufficient accuracy each lot owned by one person or company of persons, and also the names of such owners or several owners, and when he cannot ascertain the names of any such owners, or either of them, he shall state in his report, which report the Street Commissioner shall present to the City Surveyor, who shall immediately make an accurate survey, and profile of each lot or part of lot described in said report, and estimate the number of cubic yards required to fill the same, which estimate together with the profiles and said report, he shall return to the Street Commissioner who shall thereupon extend said report or assessment roll, and shall assess the owner or owners of each lot or part of lot filled, or to be filled, and when the owner or owners can not be ascertained, then such lot or part of lot shall be assessed as non-resident with the actual cost of filling the same, together with the costs and expenses of making the estimates, places and assessments incident thereto, which assessment roll together with the estimate and profiles of the City Surveyor, the Street Commissioner shall present to the Common Council, and thereupon the Controller shall advertise for fifteen days in some newspaper in said City and by posting printed notices for proposals for doing said work within such time as the Common Council shall direct and report all bids to the Common Council at their next meeting, and they shall let the contract to the lowest responsible bidder.

Duty of City Surveyor.

SEC. 6. The City Clerk shall then make out a notice directed to the several persons named in said report and proposed to be assessed, notifying them that they are about to be assessed to defray the expenses of filling up certain lots owned by them in said City, and that a report or assessment roll made out in the premises is on file in the office of said Clerk for inspection and further notifying them of the time and place when the Common Council will meet and review said assessment roll on the request of any person conceiving himself agrieved, which said notice shall be published in some paper printed in said City for four successive weeks. Duty of City Clerk.

SEC. 7. The Common Council shall at the time and place in said notice specified or at some sessions thereafter take said assessment into consideration, and if no person appears to object to said report or roll, and no good cause to the contrary appear, and an affidavit of publication of the requisite notice having been made by some one acquainted with the facts, they shall by a written resolution to be endorsed on their journal, declare that they approve of said report or assessment roll that they receive as correct the description of the lots therein mentioned and the names of the individuals therein contained, and that the same which said report states to be the correct one which each individual or set of individuals should be assessed at and pay, be the assessment, and be collected from the respective persons liable according to law; but if any sufficient cause appears or is shown to said Common Council, they shall review said report, or roll, and make such assessment as may be just and right in the premises, and said Common Council may, if necessary, adjourn from one time to any reasonable time for the purpose of finishing said review of said assessment. Common Council to consider said Assessment.

SEC. 8. Upon the conformation of the assessment roll by the Common Council, and when said lots shall have been filled up, the amount of such assessment together with all costs and charges incident to the collection thereof shall be collected in the manner prescribed for the collection of special assessments in section forty-four of title six of the Charter of the City of East Saginaw, and from the time of such conformation by the Common Council, the amount assessed upon each lot or part of lot shall be a tax and lien thereon. After confirmation amount to be a lien upon land.

CHAPTER XXXII.

OF CEMETERIES.

[Ordinance Approved July 11th, 1869].

Public Cemetery. Depth of interment.

SECTION 1. That the Cemetery known as the "Brady Hill Cemetery" is hereby declared to be the only public Cemetery within the limits of the City of East Saginaw, and the place thereof respecting lots for interment is hereby continued, and all graves shall be at least five feet deep.

Duty of the Cemetery Commissioners.—Also of the Sexton.

SEC. 2. The Commissioners of the City Cemetery shall have the care and supervision of said Cemetery, and it shall be their duty to appoint a Sexton, who shall hold his office during their pleasure, to take charge of the City hearse and when required by the friends of a deceased person or by the Director of the Poor of the said City, he shall within a reasonable time cause to be dug a grave of suitable dimensions, agreeable to the proceeding section, and shall bury the corpse therein, and when it shall be required of the Sexton, he shall deliver the coffin at the house where the corpse may be, furnish a horse for the hearse and convey the corpse to the grave.

Interments to be made in the Public Cemetery.

SEC. 3. It shall not be lawful for any person or persons to inter or cause to be intered the corpse of any deceased person in any part of said City, except in the public Cemetery aforesaid.

Sexton's fees. Provisions.

SEC. 4. The Sexton may demand and receive for his services the following fees, to wit: For opening, closing and sodding each adult's grave, three dollars; for opening, closing and sodding each child's grave, two dollars and fifty cents; for conveying a body to the Cemetery, two dollars; *Provided*, that in all cases where any other hearse than the City hearse shall be used, the Sexton shall receive for his fees in addition to the above the sum of two dollars. [*As amended by Ordinances approved May* 23, 1864 *and August* 22, 1864.

Conditions of purchasing lots.

SEC. 5. Any person who may be desirous of purchasing a lot in the public Cemetery, may make application to the Controller, and if the same be granted, the applicant shall pay the sum affixed by the Commissioners of the Cemetery to the Controller and take his certificate therefore.

SEC. 6. The purchaser or his assigns shall deposit said certificate with the City Clerk, who shall thereupon execute a deed signed by the Mayor and Clerk and countersigned by the Controller for the lot described therein and deliver the same to the person entitled thereto, and charge the Controller with the price paid. Deed.

SEC. 7. No person shall inter or cause to be intered the corpse of any deceased person in said Cemetery without the permission of the person or persons or corporation owning the lot. To prohibit interment without permission.

SEC. 8. Any person or persons who shall violate any of the provisions of this Ordinance, shall forfeit and pay a sum not exceeding twenty-five dollars with costs of suit, and if any Sexton shall neglect or refuse to perform the duties herein required, or demand for his services a sum greater than is provided by Section four of this Ordinance, he shall on conviction thereof before the Recorder's Court be fined in a sum not exceeding twenty-five dollars with costs of suit. Penalty.

SEC. 9. The Controller shall keep a Register of all lots heretofore or hereafter sold in the cemetery, by which it shall appear the name of the person or persons owning the lot, the description of the lot, the price paid therefor and the time when the deed was executed and delivered. The Controller to keep a Register.

SEC. 10. It shall not be lawful for any person to obstruct or cause to be obstructed, nor permit or suffer any obstruction occasioned by him or those under whom he claims to be or remain in any of the streets or alleys of the public Cemetery of said City, and it shall be the duty of the Sexton to remove all such obstructions at the expense of the persons, occasioning or permitting the same as aforesaid, which upon conviction shall be included in the fine adjudged against him. To prohibit the obstructing of the streets and alleys of the Public Cemetery.

SEC. 11. The Commissioners of the Cemetery shall, whenever necessary, designate suitable lots in the public Cemetery for the interment of the corpse of any deceased poor person or stranger, and it shall be the duty of the Sexton to inter any such corpse in any lot so designated. Provision for the interment of strangers, etc.

SEC. 12. It shall be the duty of the Sexton to keep a Register of all interment made in the public Cemetery in which shall be Sexton to keep a Register.

stated the name of the deceased, his late residence, the place of his birth, his occupation and the disease or complaint of which he died, and, at the expiration of every quarter, report the same to the Common Council and the Cemetery Commissioners and cause a copy thereof to be published in the City newspaper. The Sexton shall also, at the expiration of his term of office, deliver said Register to his successor in office, or to the Commissioners of the Cemetery.

Receiving tomb to be provided. Streets and alleys to be graded.

SEC. 13. The Commissioners of the Cemetery when directed by the Common Council shall cause to be provided a receiving tomb, and it shall be their duty to cause the streets and alleys of the Cemetery to be graded and worked and such other improvements of said Cemetery grounds as may be for the best intersts of the City.

Rules and Regulations to be annexed to deeds.

SEC. 14. Rules and Regulations to be annexed to deeds.

1st. Lots shall not be used for any other purpose than as a place of burial for the dead.

2d. Proprietors shall not allow interments to be made in their lots for a remuneration.

3d. The proprietor of each lot shall have a right to enclose the same with a hedge or with a fence or railing of stone, marble or iron, not over three feet high, all such railing or fence should be neat and symmetrical.

4th. The proprietor of each lot shall also have the right to erect any proper stones, monuments or sepulchral structure thereon, and to cultivate trees, shrubs and plants in the same; but no tree growing within the lots or border shall be cut down or destroyed without the consent of the Superintendents.

Change.

5th. If any trees or shrubs situated in any lot shall by means of their roots, branches or otherwise become detrimental to the adjacent lots or avenues, or dangerous, or inconvenient to passengers, it shall be the duty of the Superintendents and they shall have the right to enter the said lot and remove the said trees and shrubs or such parts thereof as are detrimental, dangerous or inconvenient.

6th. If any monument or effigy or any structure whatever of any description be placed in or upon any lot which shall be determined by the Common Council to be offensive or improper, the Superintendents shall have the right and it shall be their duty to enter upon such lot and remove the said offensive or improper object or objects.

7th. No disinterment shall be allowed without permission from the Superintendents.

CHAPTER XXXIII.

OF NUISANCES.

[Ordinance Approved July 18th, 1870.]

SECTION 1. No person or persons within the City shall permit or suffer on his, her or their premises, or any premises which he she or they may be occupants, any nuisance, nor shall he, she or they exercise any calling or trade which is unwholesome or offensive by which a nuisance shall be created, by offensive and nauseous stench or otherwise, which shall or may become offensive or dangerous to the neighborhood or travelers. No person shall suffer any nuisances to exist on premises occupied by him.

SEC. 2. No person shall, himself or by another, throw, place, deposit or leave in any street, highway, lane, alley, space or square, any animal or vegetable substance, dead animal, fish, shells, shavings, dirt, rubbish, excrement, filth, odor, slops, unclean or nauseous water or liquor, hay, straw, ashes, cinders, soot, offal, garbage swill or any other article or substance whatever, which may cause any noisome, offensive or unwholesome smell. Nuisances in streets and public places prohibited.

SEC. 3. No distiller, soap boiler, tallow chandler, dyer, machinist or other person, shall himself or by another, discharge out of or from any still house, soap or candle factory, dye-house, work shop, factory, machine shop, dwelling house, kitchen or other building, any foul or nauseous liquid, water or other substance, into or upon any highway, street, lane, alley, public space or square, or into any adjacent lot or ground. Discharges from Still House, etc. prohibited.

Nuisances in private houses, etc. prohibited.

SEC. 4. No person shall keep, place, or have on or in any private house, lot or premises in this City, any dead carcase, putrid, offensive or unsound beef, pork, fish, hide, skins, bones, horns, stinking or rotten soap, grease, tallow, offal, garbage or other animal or vegetable matter or substances, which may cause any unwholesome, noisome or offensive smell.

Nuisances in groceries, etc. prohibited.

SEC. 5. No owner or occupant of any grocery, cellar, tallow chandler's shop, soap, candle, starch, or glue factory, tannery, butcher shop, slaughter house, stable, barn, privy, sewer or other building or place, shall allow any nuisance to exist or remain on his or her premises.

Livery stables to be kept clean.

SEC. 6. The keeper of any livery or other stable, shall keep the stable and yard clean, and shall not permit, between the first day of June and the first day of November, more than two cart loads of manure to accumulate in or near the same at any one time.

Places for slaughtering to be paved and cleaned.

SEC. 7. Every person slaughtering beeves, sheep or other animals within the City limits, shall cause the house, yard or place, where such killing is done, to be provided with a tight plank floor, or to be paved with brick or stone, and if paved, the earth below, shall be sufficiently solid to prevent it becoming the receptacle of the filthy or offensive matter; such floor or pavement shall be so constructed as to carry off into a tub or reservoir all blood and offal. At the end of each day, when killing is done on the premises, the same shall be thoroughly washed and cleansed, and the tubs or vessels containing the blood and offal emptied.

Slaughtering houses to be whitewashed.

SEC. 8. Every slaughter house in this City shall be whitewashed inside, at least once in each month, between the first day of April and the first day of November.

Hides not to remain in streets.

SEC. 9. No person shall allow any green or salted hides to remain on any street, sidewalk or other open place within this City, longer than one hour.

Offensive hand bills, etc. not to be posted.

SEC. 10. No person shall himself, or by another, paste or put up, or cause to be put up, or displayed in any conspicuous place, or on any lamp posts, fences, posts, boxes, sidewalks, bridges or buildings within the City, any card or hand bill, advertising any obscene books, shows, amusements, cuts, pictures, resorts or the place or means of curing syphilistic or other secret diseases.

Hand bills not to be posted on public buildings, etc.

SEC. 11. No person shall place, or in any manner fasten, any placard, show bill or advertisement, upon or against any public buildings, or any part thereof, or against any fence or enclosures belonging to the City of East Saginaw.

Hogs not to be collected, etc.

SEC. 12. No person shall collect or confine hogs in pens or otherwise, so as to become offensive to his or their neighbor or neighbors; nor shall such person keep or use any hog pen, privy or barn yard adjoining to and abutting on any lot, upon which any person resides, or so near or in a position thereto, that the contents of said hog pen or privy, or barn yard are discharged upon such lot.

Nuisances on docks, etc. prohibited.

SEC. 13. No person shall place, deposit, throw or keep in any dock or wharf, or in the water of the Saginaw River, within the City limits, any straw, hay, green boughs, cord wood, vegetables, perishable substance, excrement, carcass, bones, horns, shells, meats, hides, offal, garbage or any unwholesome or decayed matter or anything whatever.

Privies to be maintained.

SEC. 14. Every dwelling house, store, manufactory or shop hereafter built in the City of East Saginaw, shall be provided with a suitable privy, the vault of which shall be walled up with two inch plank, brick or stone, and be sunk at least five feet below the level of the earth for any private house, and at least ten feet for any public or boarding house. The inside of such vault shall be at least one foot distant from the line of every adjoining highway, street, lane, alley, or lot, and when there is a public sewer within one hundred feet of such privy, it shall be so constructed as to be drained into such sewer. In cases where privies or outhouses are already built, the owner or occupant shall be required to rebuild the same as above provided whenever the Board of Health shall so order, the change to be made within twenty days after the service of the proper notice upon the owner or occupant from said Board.

Constructi'n of privies.

SEC. 15. The Mayor and Aldermen of the City, and members of the Board of Health, shall have power, and it is hereby made their, and each of their duty, upon being satisfied that any store, manufactory, shop or dwelling house, as aforesaid, is not provided with a suitable privy, as provided in the last section, to notify in writing, the owner or occupant of such dwelling to construct such a privy within twenty days within the date of the service of such notice, and if such owner or occupant of such dwelling neglect or refuse to comply with the requirements of such notice within the time specified, the Common Council may cause a suitable privy to be constructed for such dwelling house, and the expense thereof shall be charged as a special tax or assessment, on the dwelling house and the ground attached thereto, to be levied and collected in the same manner as other assessments imposed by authority of the Common Council, as provided in title 10, section 9, of the act to incorporate the City of East Saginaw.

Emptying of privies.

SEC. 16. No privy shall be emptied between the first day of June and the first day of September, unless by the written permission of the Mayor or of the Board of Health. Privies shall be emptied between the hours of ten P M. and 3 A. M., and at no other time.

Swill carts to be covered.

SEC. 17. Any cart, wagon, or other vehicle used or intended to be used for the purpose of conveying swill, offal, garbage, excrement, odor or night-soil, shall be perfectly tight, and covered so as to prevent the contents thereof from leaking or spilling, and such cart, wagon or other vehicle, when not in use, shall not be allowed to stand in any highway, street, lane, alley, public space or square.

Penalty.

SEC. 18. Any violation of the provisions of this Ordinance shall be punished by a fine not exceeding one hundred dollars and costs of prosecution, and in the imposition of any fine and costs the court may make a further sentence, that the offender be imprisoned in the county jail or City prison until payment thereof. *Provided, however*, the period of imprisonment shall not exceed the term of ninety days.

SEC. 19. An Ordinance entitled "An Ordinance relative to nuisances," made and passed July 11th, 1859, and an ordinance entitled "An Ordinance relative to nuisances," made and passed May 21, 1866, be and the same are hereby repealed.

TITLE VI.

OF THE PUBLIC PEACE.

CHAPTER XXXIV.

OF THE PUBLIC PEACE.

[Ordinance Approved June 27th, 1870.]

SECTION 1. Any person found lying in wait, lurking or concealed in any building or premises, with intent to do mischief, pilfer or commit crime or misdemeanor, shall be punished as hereinafter provided. *Lying in wait prohibited.*

SEC. 2. Any person or persons who shall make or assist in making any noise, disturbance or improper diversion, or any rout or riot by which the peace and good order of the neighborhood are disturbed, shall be punished as hereinafter provided. *Disturbance's etc., prohibited.*

SEC. 3. All vagrants, mendicants and drunken or disorderly persons, shall be punished as hereinafter provided. *Vagrancy, etc., prohibited.*

SEC. 4. No person shall be guilty of any indecent or immoral language, conduct, or behavior to any person or persons in any street, lane, alley or elsewhere in said City. *Indecent language and behavior prohibited.*

SEC. 5. Any person who shall by talking, laughing or otherwise interrupt the service in any place of divine worship, shall be punished as hereinafter provided. *Disturbance's in places of worship prohibited.*

Crowds in front of churches prohibited.

SEC 6 Persons shall not collect or stand in crowds in front of any church or place of worship during service.

Indecent exposures prohibited.

SEC. 7. No person shall make any indecent exposure of his or her person in the streets, lanes, alleys, markets or public places of said City.

Sales of obscene pictures and books prohibited.

SEC. 8. No person shall show, sell or offer for sale, or exhibit any indecent or obscene picture, drawing, engraving, book or pamphlet.

Penalty.

SEC. 9. Any violation of the provisions of this Ordinance shall be punished by a fine not exceeding one hundred dollars and costs, and in the imposition of any fine and costs, the court may make a further sentence that the offender be committed to the City prison or county jail, until such fine and costs are paid. *Provided, however*, that the term of such imprisonment shall not exceed the period of thirty days.

CHAPTER XXXV.

OF DISORDERLY PERSONS.

[Ordinance Approved July 11th, 1859.]

Prohibit riots, etc.

SECTION 1. Any person who shall make, aid, countenance or assist in making any noise, riot or disturbance, or improper diversion, who shall be guilty of any indecent, criminal or insulting conduct or language in the streets or elsewhere in this City, and all persons who shall collect in bodies or crowds in said City, for unlawful purposes to the annoyance or disturbance of citizens or travelers, shall on conviction thereof, before the Recorder's court, or any Justice of the Peace of the City be fined to the use of said City, in a sum not more than one hundred dollars nor less than three dollars.

Penalty.

To prohibit threats and intoxication.

SEC. 2. Every person who shall threaten to beat or kill another, or to injure him in his person or his property, or who shall contend with hot and angry words to the disturbance of the peace or who shall be intoxicated in the streets or any other place in said City, shall be liable to the punishment prescribed in the foregoing section.

SEC. 3. Any person violating the provisions of the two preceding sections or any of them may be arrested by the Marshal, City or Police Constable, or by any person ordered so to do by any member of the Common Council without process and taken before the Recorder's court or any Justice of the Peace of said City who shall thereupon proceed to hear and determine the same: *Provided*, that any person arrested as aforesaid may demand and have a trial by jury, and *Provided further*, that no such arrest shall be made without process unless the offence be committed in the presence of Marshal, City or Police Constable, or of some member of the Council.

How arrested.

Provisions for trial.

SEC. 4. The Recorder's court or any Justice of the Peace of the City may issue a warrant or capias for the arrest of any person or persons charged on oath with having violated any of the provisions of this Ordinance, and on the return of said warrant the said court or Justice may hear and determine the case.

Warrant or capias for arrest;—how issued.

SEC. 5. The Recorder or Justice before whom any person may be brought charged with violating any of the provisions of this Ordinance, may also in his discretion require said person to give surety for his good behaviour for the term of one year in such sum and with such security as said Recorder or Justice may approve, and said surety bond shall be filed by the person taking the same within ten days with the City Attorney, and in case of forfeiture, be prosecuted by him in behalf of the City.

Security for good behavior may be required

SEC. 6. In case any person shall neglect or refuse to pay any fine imposed under this Ordinance or to give surety for his good behavior within such time as shall be prescribed by the Recorder or the Justice as aforesaid, said Recorder or Justice may by warrant under his hand commit said person so neglecting or refusing to the City prison or common jail of Saginaw county until he shall pay said fine or give such surety; *Provided*, that said imprisonment shall not in any case exceed ninety days. The warrant of commitment may be executed by the Marshal of the City or any Constable of said county.

Provisions for imprisonment.

CHAPTER XXXVI.

OF CLOSING CERTAIN PLACES ON THE SABBATH.

[Ordinance Approved May 15th, 1865.]

Closing of saloons, etc. on the Sabbath.

Section 1. It shall not hereafter be lawful to keep open within the limits of said City on the first day of the week called Sunday, any show, theatre, saloon, dance house, place of amusement or other place of business in said City, where intoxicating drinks shall be kept for sale.

Penalty.

Sec. 2. Whoever shall violate the preceding section shall on conviction be fined not less than five nor more than fifty dollars and on failure to pay such fine shall be imprisonment in the county jail of Saginaw county or the City prison not less than ten nor more than thirty days.

CHAPTER XXXVII.

OF PUBLIC DECENCY.

[Ordinance Approved July 11th, 1859.]

To regulate public bathing, etc.

Section 1. If any person or persons shall by bathing or otherwise expose his or their naked bodies, within the limits of said City, between the hours of four o'clock in the forenoon and nine o'clock in the afternoon, he or they shall, upon conviction thereof, pay a fine not less than one dollar nor more than twenty dollars, and in default of payment shall be imprisoned in the City prison or in the county jail for not less than one day nor more than twenty days.

Penalty.

To prohibit the use of fire arms on Sunday.

Sec. 2. It shall not be lawful for any one on the first day of the week called Sunday, to fire any gun, rifle or pistol for sport, diversion or otherwise within the limits of said City, and whoever shall violate the provisions of this section, shall be liable to the penalty imposed in the last preceding section of every offence.

Penalty.

CHAPTER XXXVIII.

OF THE SALE OF LIQUOR ON ELECTION DAY.

[Ordinance Approved May 16th, 1870.]

SECTION 1. No person shall sell, or give away, or expose for sale, any intoxicating liquors, or keep open any saloon, grocery, bar or other place, for the purpose of selling, giving away or exposing for sale, any intoxicating liquor during the day of any election, held in this City, for municipal, State or National purposes. No person shall sell, etc. on election day.

SEC. 2. That in any prosecution under this Ordinance, it shall not be necessary to aver or prove the particular kind of liquor sold or given away, or exposed for sale; but it shall be sufficient to aver and prove the same to be intoxicating liquors. Evidence under.

SEC. 3. That any person violating the provisions of this Ordinance, shall, on conviction thereof, be fined not less than five nor more than twenty dollars, and in default of the payment of the fine and costs, may be imprisoned in the City prison or county jail for a term not exceeding twenty days, in the discretion of the court. Penalty.

CHAPTER XXXIX.

OF HOUSES OF ILL FAME.

[Ordinance Approved May 16th, 1870.]

SECTION 1. No occupant or owner of any premises within the City shall keep, or suffer to be kept on said premises, a house of ill fame. No person shall keep house of ill fame.

SEC. 2. No person shall reside in a house of ill fame, or visit such house for the purpose of prostitution, and if any person shall be found visiting any house of ill fame, it shall be *prima faica* evidence of having visited it for that purpose; but such person may exculpate himself or herself by reasonable proof. Living in or visiting such houses prohibited.

SEC. 3. If it shall appear on the trial of any cause under this Ordinance, that the general reputation of the house is that of a house of ill fame, it shall be *prima facia* evidence that such house is a house of ill fame within the meaning of this Ordinance, but any person may exculpate himself or herself by reasonable proof.

Penalty.

SEC. 4. Any person who shall violate the provisions of this Ordinance, shall be punished by a fine not exceeding one hundred dollars and the costs of prosecution, and in the imposition of any such fine and costs the court may make a further sentence that in default of the payment thereof, such offender be imprisoned in the county jail of Saginaw county, or the City prison, for a period of time, not exceeding thirty days.

TITLE VII.

OF THE RECORDER'S COURT.

CHAPTER XL.

OF PROCESS AND PROCEEDINGS IN RECORDER'S COURT.

[Ordinance Approved August 1st, 1870.]

SECTION 1. Upon complaint on oath or affirmation being made to the Clerk of the Recorder's Court, that any person who has violated any of the laws or Ordinances of said City, the Clerk shall issue a capias *ad respondendum* unless a summons be specially prescribed for the arrest of such person, and shall be returnable forthwith, or at the present or ensuing term of said court. When process may be issued from Recorder's Court.

SEC. 2. Before issuing such process, the Clerk may, if he shall deem it necessary, require the complainant to enter into a bond with sufficient surety to the City of East Saginaw, conditioned for the appearance of the complainant at the term of the Recordor's Court, at which such person shall be made returnable to give evidence against the person or persons complained of by him, and if upon trial the defendant shall be discharged, that the complainants shall pay the costs of prosecution, if so ordered by the said court, and in his discretion, said Clerk may require a sum not exceeding five dollars to be deposited with him by the complainant to be applied to the payment of the costs in case the complainant is so ordered to pay the same. When security for costs may be required.

Who to execute process.

SEC. 3. It shall be the duty of the Marshal or Constable to whom the writ shall be directed, to arrest the defendant therein named if he be found, who may give bail for his appearance at the time such writ shall be returnable, and in default thereof the officer shall take him before any member of the Common Council, who may commit, let to bail or discharge the defendant according to his discretion.

Bond upon arrest.

SEC. 4. The bail required in the preceding section shall be by bond, payable to the City of East Saginaw, with at least one sufficient surety in a sum not less than twenty-five dollars and not more than double the amount of penalty provided in the By-Laws or Ordinances which may be violated, and shall be conditioned for the due appearance of the defendant before the Recorder's Court, and not depart without leave, and in the meantime keep the peace toward all good people of said City. *Provided*, That if such bail should be insufficient or irresponsible, the officer taking the same shall be liable in an action of debt for the amount thereof, to be recovered in the name of the City.

Execution to issue against body, goods and real estate.

SEC. 5. Executions returnable at the next term may issue upon any judgment of the said court against the body, goods and chattels of the defendants or party prosecuted (unless such party be in actual custody for the offense on which judgment was rendered) for the amount of such fine and the costs of prosecution, which execution may be levied upon the goods and chattels or body of such party; and all goods and chattels so levied upon shall be sold in the same manner, in all respects, that personal property is directed by the laws of this State to be sold, except that six days previous notice shall be sufficient and the officer levying the same shall return the execution at the next term of the Recorder's Court with his doings thereon; and if such execution be returned unsatisfied in whole or in part, an execution may be issued against the real estate of such defendant, which shall be executed according to the laws of this State.

When complainant to pay costs.

SEC. 6. If in any trial it shall appear to the court, that the complaint was wilful or malicious, or without probable cause, or if the complainant does not appear and testify in the cause, the court may order and adjudge the complainant (and if he has entered into a bond as required by this Ordinance, then him and his surety) to pay the costs of such prosecution, and thereupon an execution as in other cases shall issue for the same But if a deposit in money shall be made, such costs shall be paid therefrom and no execution shall issue. In all cases the surplus of any money deposited for costs after the payment of such costs shall be returned by said Clerk to the complainant.

Constable's and Marshal's return

SEC. 7. The Marshal and Constable once in each month and whenever it can be done, at least three days prior to the term of the Recorder's Court shall return to the clerk of said court all process issued out of said court, with their doings in each case endorsed thereon, and shall also at such times pay over all moneys collected by them in pursuance of such process to the said clerk; and if any such officer shall neglect or refuse to comply with the provisions af this section, or shall knowingly do any other act inconsistent with the just and faithful discharge of his duties, he shall, on conviction, be liable to pay a penalty not exceeding one hundred dollars and costs of prosecution.

Clerk to report monthly to Council.

SEC. 8. The Clerk shall receive all fines and costs that are paid without the issuing of process for collection, and he shall once in each month make report to the Common Council of all the particulars and business of the Recorder's Court; the number of persons tried and the amount of fines and costs of each term, and the amount collected and paid into his hands, and he shall immediately pay over to the City Treasurer, all moneys by him received, belonging to the City, together with all witness or juror's fees on hand and shall take from the Treasurer a receipt therefor, which when presented to and countersigned by the Controller shall be a sufficient voucher to said Clerk for such payments.

Penalty for obstructing officers.

SEC. 9. If any person or persons knowingly or wilfully obstruct, resist or oppose the Marshal or any of the Constables of said City, or other person or persons duly authorized in serving or attempting to serve any writ or process, rule or order issued out of said Recorder's Court, or while executing or carrying into effect any order, rule or determination of the Common Council of said City, or shall resist or impede any person duly authorized, or any member of the Common Council of said City, in the performance of any of their duties or powers, or if any person shall aid or assist any person legally in custody, to escape or conceal him after the escape every person offending in the premises shall on conviction before said Recorder's Court be punished by a fine not exceeding one hundred dollars and costs.

Duty of officers when it is not convenient to bring persons before Recorder, etc.

SEC. 10. If any officer shall arrest any person at a time that may be inconvenient to bring him before any proper officer for examination, the officer making the arrest may place such person in the custody of the keeper of the City prison, and within fifteen hours thereafter, he shall bring him before some of the Police Justices, the Recorder or some other member of the Common Council for examination, and if such officer shall neglect to comply with the requirements of this section, he shall be liable to pay all the expenses of keeping such prisoner in the City prison. *Provided*, That if the said period of fifteen hours shall terminate on the Sabbath day, said examination shall be during the forenoon of the next ensuing Monday.

Duty of Jailor.

SEC. 11. The keeper of the City prison shall not permit or suffer any person committed by virtue of a process of the Recorder's Court or other authority of the City to leave or depart from said City prison, without the permission in writing of some member of the Common Council, Mayor or the City Attorney, under a penalty of a sum not exceeding one hundred dollars and costs of prosecution.

Court may require convicted persons to give recognizance for good behavior.

SEC. 12. Whenever any person is convicted before the Recorder's Court of any offense against the Ordinances of the City, it shall be competent for the court to require from the party so convicted a recognizance with sufficient surety or sureties in such sum as the court shall direct, conditional for his or her good behavior for a period not exceeding one year, and any violation of the Ordinance under which the party was convicted shall be deemed a breach of such recognizance. The court may also order such party to be committed to the house of correction till such recognizance is given.

CHAPTER XLI.

OF FEES IN RECORDER'S COURT.

[Ordinance Approved August 1st, 1870.]

SECTION. 1. The Recorder, officers or jurors for duties performed in the Recorder's Court, in street opening and City Ordinance cases, shall receive the following fees: Fees.

1st. For serving a warrant or other process for the arrest of any person, fifty cents. For serving process.

2d For serving a subpœna, thirteen cents. For serving Suphœna.

3d. For each person taken to prison or final commitment, thirteen cents. For Commitment.

4th. For arrests made without process, provided the court shall determine that such arrest was for probable crime, fifty cents. For arrest.

5th. For every mile actually and necessarily traveled beyond the City in serving process, six cents. For travel.

6th. For each day's attendance as a juror in the trial of cases, one dollar and fifty cents and seventy-five cents for each half day. For attending as Jurors.

7th. For every day actually and necessarily employed as a juror in the matter of opening, widening, extending or vacating streets, alleys, &c., one dollar and fifty cents, and for each half day actually and necessarily employed, seventy-five cents. For attending as Juror in street opening case

8th. For every day actually and necessarily employed as Recorder in holding court in the matter of opening, widening, extending or vacating streets, alleys, &c., four dollars, and for each half day actually and necessarily employed, one dollar and a half. For the Recorder.

9th. For every day actually and necessarily employed by the Clerk, attending the actual settings of the Recorder's Court, in opening, widening, extending or vacating streets, alleys, &c., one dollar and fifty cents, and for each half day actually and necessarily employed, seventy-five cents. For Clerk.

10th. For performing the duties prescribed in Sec. 3, Title 4, of the City Charter, the Marshal shall receive ten cents for each notice served as required by said Section. For Marshal

SEC. 2. No fees shall be paid to witnesses. No fees to witnesses

Fees may be required in advance.

SEC. 3. Officers serving process for a defendant may demand and receive his fees in advance.

Clerk to deliver over books and papers to his successor.

SEC. 4. The Clerk of said Court, at the end of each term thereof, shall deliver to each officer and juror, a certificate specifying the services of such officer or juror, and the amount due him; such services together with the Recorder's fees, shall be certified and sworn to before the City Controller and paid for by the City in the same manner as other claims and demands against the corporation. *Provided, however*, That the Clerk of said court shall have the right to swear the foreman or any member of the jury in the matter of opening, widening, vacating or extending a street, alley, &c., as to the time actually and necessarily employed by such jury.

TITLE VIII.

PREVENTION AND EXTINGUISHMENT OF FIRES.

CHAPTER XLII.

OF THE FIRE DEPARTMENT.

[Ordinance Approved July 11th, 1859.]

SECTION 1. The fire department of said City shall consist of a Chief Engineer, an Assistant Engineer and as many other engineers, fire wardens, fire engine men, hose men, hook and ladder men, axe men and bag men as may from time to time be appointed by the Common Council and who shall be respectively distinguished by the appellations aforesaid. Who shall constitute Fire Department.

SEC. 2. The Chief and Assistant Engineers and two or more Fire Wardens for this City, when nominated by the fire department, may be appointed by the Common Council in the month of April in each year, or at such other time or times as the Common Council shall determine. The members of the Common Council of this City shall be *ex-officio* fire wardens, and a fire warden, (except those who are *ex-officio* fire wardens) shall be assigned and attached by the Mayor to each company of fire men having charge of a fire engine as he shall think proper, and at every fire every Warden shall report himself to the Chief Engineer and be subject to his directions and to the directions of the other Engineers of the fire department, and it shall be the duty of said Fire Wardens to prevent the hose being trodden on and to keep all idle and Appointme't of Chief and Assistant Engineers.

suspected persons from the fire and its vicinity, and also to use all proper exertions within their power for the preservation of goods and other property endangered at fires, and all citizens are hereby enjoined and required to comply with the directions of said Fire Wardens, provided such directions be not in opposition to the orders of the person having supreme control at said fire.

Duties of Engineers.

SEC. 3. All the said Engineers, on an alarm of fire, shall immediately repair to the place where the same is, and report themselves to the Chief Engineer or person having command of the fire department for the time being under a penalty for every wilful neglect not exceeding fifty dollars.

Power of Chief Engineer.

SEC. 4. The Chief Engineer shall have full power, control and command over all persons whatever, at any fire, except members of the Common Council, and in his absence the Assistant Engineer shall perform his duties. In the absence of all the Engineers the Mayor or in his absence any member of the Common Council may designate some person to discharge the said duties until the proper officer may arrive.

Duty of the Chief Engineer.

SEC. 5. It shall be the duty of the Chief Engineer to direct at all fires all such measures as he may deem most advisable for the effectual extinguishment of the said fires, and also once in every six months to examine the condition of the fire engines and other apparatus, together with the engine houses belonging to the corporation and report the same to the Common Council accompanied by the names and number of all the members of the fire department and the respective associations to which they belong which shall be annually published in the month of December by the Clerk of said City in such newspaper of said City, as shall be employed by the Common Council, and whenever any of the said fire engines or other fire apparatus shall require to be repaired, the Chief Engineer shall cause the same to be well and sufficiently done, and he shall report in writing all accidents of fire that may happen in this City with the cause thereof as well as can be ascertained and the number and descriptions of the buildings destroyed or injured, together with the names of the owners and occupants to the Clerk, who shall keep a faithful register of the same.

SEC. 6. The fire engine men shall be divided into companies to consist of as many members as the Common Council shall direct, one of which companies to be assigned to each of the fire engines belonging or that may hereafter belong to the City, and that each of the said companies shall and may choose out of their number a Foreman, Assistant and Clerk in such manner and at such times as they may think proper, and it shall be the duty of said fire engine men as often as any fire shall brake out in said City, to repair immediately upon the alarm thereof to their respective fire engines and convey them to or near the place where such fire shall happen, and in conformity with the directions given by the Chief Engineer or Engineers shall work and manage the said fire engine, hose and other implements and instruments thereunto belonging, with all their skill and power, and when the fire is extinguished, shall not remove therefrom but by the direction of the Chief Engineer or of the other Engineers, which direction being obtained, they shall return with their respective fire engines and with the hose and other implements to their several places of deposit, and as soon as may be thereafter wash and clean the same and for the more effectually keeping and preserving the fire engines from decay, the said fire engine men, when the season of the year will permit, shall by order of the Chief Engineer draw out the said fire engines in order to wash, cleanse and exercise them, and if any fire engine man shall neglect said duty, he shall forfeit or pay for every default one dollar, and if he shall neglect to attend any fire as aforesaid or leave his fire engine while at any fire, without permission, or not perform his duty on such occasion without reasonable excuse, he shall for every default forfeit and pay a sum not exceeding five dollars and also to be removed and displaced from his station.

Division of Fire Engine men.

SEC. 7. The hose, hook, ladder, axe and bag men shall be divided into companies to consist of as many members as the Common Council shall direct, and each company shall choose out of their number a Foreman, Assistant and Clerk in such manner and at such times as they may think proper, and it shall be the duty of such hose, hook, ladder, axe and bag men to cause their hose, hooks, ladders and other implements to be conveyed to the place

Division of hose, hook, ladder, axe and bag men

where any fire may happen, and to apply and use the same agreeable to such directions as they may receive from the Chief Engineer or other Engineers, and after such fire shall be extinguished to return the same when dismissed by the Chief Engineers to the place where they are usually deposited and as soon as may be thereafter, wash and cleanse the same, and if any hose, hook, ladder, axe or engine man shall wilfully neglect to perform any of the duties aforesaid, he shall forfeit a sum not exceeding five dollars for every such neglect and also be removed from his displaced station.

Certificate of appointment to be countersig'd by the Clerk within one month from election.

SEC. 8. Whenever any fire engine man, hose, hook, ladder, axe and bag man is elected member of any fire company or to supply any vacancy therein, it shall be his duty to call upon the Treasurer of the fire department and procure a certificate within one month from the date of his election countersigned by the Clerk, specifying the name and number of the company to which such fire engine man, hose, hook, ladder, axe and bag man shall be elected, and if any fire engine man, hose, hook, ladder, axe and bag man whose office from any cause may become vacant shall be re-elected, he shall take up a new certificate as aforesaid and it shall be the duty of the Chief Engineer to certify on each certificate whenever any vacancy exists in the company to which any fire engine man, hose, hook, ladder, axe and bag man shall be elected as aforesaid, and if such certificate shall not be procured within the time above prescribed such appointment shall be null and void.

Badge of office of the members of the Common Council.

SEC. 9. The members of the Common Council shall severally bear a staff with a gilded frame at the top and shall not be required to bear any other badge of office.

Chief Engineer shall wear badge and carry trumpet.

SEC. 10. The Chief Engineer shall wear a painted leather cap with the words "Chief Engineer" painted on the frontis piece thereof, and shall also carry a bright speaking trumpet with the words "Chief Engineer" painted thereon.

Also Assistant Engineers.

SEC. 11. The Assistant Engineers shall wear painted leather caps with the words "Engine No. 1," or "Engine No. 2," painted on the frontis piece thereof. They shall also carry a speaking trumpet with the works "Engine No. 1," or "Engine No. 2," painted thereon.

SEC. 12. The fire wardens shall severally wear a hat and the word "Warden" painted on the frontis piece thereof, and shall also carry a staff with the word "Warden" painted thereon.

Fire Wardens shall wear a hat appropriately marked and carry staff.

SEC. 13. The Foreman and Assistant Foreman of the engine, hose, hook and ladder companies and the members of said companies shall wear such caps as shall be prescribed by the companies, and the said caps shall be distinguished in the manner following, viz: The cap of each foreman shall have the word "Foreman" painted on the frontis piece of the same, together with the number of the engine or company to which he may belong, and each member of an engine, hose or hook and ladder company shall have the number of the engine or company to which he belongs painted upon the frontis piece of his cap.

Cap of the Foreman, Assistant Foreman and each member of the fire companies.

SEC. 14. All persons who at a fire shall refuse to obey any order or direction given by a person duly authorized to order or direct, or who shall resist or impede any officer or other person in the discharge of his duty shall in the absence of sufficient excuse be punished by a fine not exceeding fifty dollars, and any member of the Common Council may cause such person to be arrested and detained in custody until such fire is extinguished and such person shall then be liable to be prosecuted for such fine before any court having cognizance thereof.

Penalty for disobedience of orders at fires.

SEC. 15. It shall be lawful for the Foreman or Assistant Foreman of any fire engine or other fire company or for any member of the Common Council, Chief Engineer or Assistant to require the aid of any citizen or inhabitant in drawing any engine or other apparatus to the fire, and on neglect or refusal to comply with such requisition the offender shall pay the penalty of five dollars.

Penalty for refusing to help draw any engine or other apparatus to fires.

SEC. 16. If any person shall wilfully injure in any manner any hose, fire engine or other apparatus or building containing the same belonging to the City, the offender shall for every such offence forfeit and pay the sum of twenty dollars, besides being liable to an action for the recovery of the damages done.

SEC. 17. The Marshal and every constable shall repair immediately on the alarm of fire with their staff of office to the place where the fire may be and report himself to any member of the Common Council for the preservation of the public peace and the removal of all idle and suspected persons or the preservation of property in the vicinity of the fire, and if the Marshal or any Constable shall neglect to comply with the prvisions of this section, he shall pay a fine not exceeding fifty dollars and be subject to removal from office.

SEC. 18. The hook and ladder men and axe men shall under the direction of the Chief Engineer, and two members of the Common Council present or in the absence of the Chief Engineer, then under the direction of the Assistant Engineer and two members of the Common Council, or in the absence of all the Engineers then under the direction of any three of the Common Council if so many be present, cut down and remove any building, erection or fence for the purpose of checking the progress of the fire.

SEC. 19. Semi-annually in the months of March and September, all fines provided by this or the Ordinance relative to the prevention of fires shall enure to the benefit of the fire department when collected after deducting all costs and expenses incurred in the prosecution thereof, and any specified sum as a fine may be paid by the person liable therefor to such of the Fire Wardens as shall be designated by the Common Council and such Fire Wardens shall note in a book to be furnished by the Common Council all violations of this and the Ordinance relative to the prevention of fires and make an annual report thereof to the Treasurer of the fire department, and the said Fire Wardens shall also pay all moneys received by them by virtue of this section to such Collector as shall be specially designated by the Common Council for that purpose.

SEC. 20. If any person having charge of any engine or other fire apparatus shall suffer or permit the same to be applied to private uses without the consent of the Mayor, Chief Engineer or Common Council, he shall forfeit the penalty of five dollars together with the damages occasioned thereto.

CHAPTER XLIII.

OF THE PREVENTION OF FIRES.

[Ordinance Approved July 22d, 1861.]

SECTION 1. The following boundaries shall constitute and be known as the fire limits of the City of East Saginaw, to wit: Water Blocks Nos. 4 and 5, and Blocks Nos. 17, 18, 19, 20, 34 and 35, and Lots Nos. 1, 2, 3, 4, 5 and 6 in Block No. 33; Lots Nos. 1, 2, 3, 4, 5 and 6 in Block No. 36; Lots Nos. 1, 2, 3, 4, 5, 6, 10, 11 and 12 in Block No. 44; Lots Nos. 1, 2, 3, 4, 5, 6, 7, 8 and 9 in Block No. 45; Lots Nos. 1, 2, 3, 10, 11 and 12 in Block No. 59; Lots Nos. 4, 5, 6, 7, 8 and 9 in Block No. 58; Lots Nos. 1, 2, 3, 10, 11 and 12 in Block No. 66; and entire Block No. 67, all in and as designated upon Hoyt's Plat of the City of East Saginaw. [*As Amended by Ordinance Approved January* 16, 1866. Fire limits.

SEC. 2. No person shall erect or place any building, shed, store-house or other erection, or part of any building, shed or store-house or other erection, within said fire limits, unless the same shall be constructed of stone or brick with partition walls, fire-proof roofs, brick, iron or stone cornices, iron, stone or brick columns, and metalic eave troughs, and if wooden timbers are used for the support of the front wall over the columns, the same shall be protected by stone, brick or iron at least four inches thick in front, and eight inches at each end, and in all buildings erected of stone or brick, in blocks of two or more buildings, in said fire limits, there shall be entire brick partition walls running at right angles with the streets upon which such buildings shall front, or as nearly so as the plan of the City will admit, at least one foot in thickness, and extending at least three feet above the roof. [*As Amended by Ordinance Approved Jan.* 16, 1866.] Method and plan of erecting buildings.

SEC. 3. Nothing contained in the preceeding Section shall prohibit the erection within said fire limits of any wooden building not more than five feet square and ten feet in height from the ground to the peak of the roof. *Provided*, That nothing in this Section shall be construed so as to allow the placing of two or more wooden buildings adjoining or adjacent to each other. Size of wooden building limited.

Consent of Common Council to repair buildings partially destroyed by fire.

SEC. 4. No person shall, except as is provided in sections five and six of this Ordinance, repair any wooden building within said fire limits, without the consent of the Common Council, nor elevate from the ground, or in any way increase the height of, or remove any such building from any lot within said fire limits, to any other lot within said fire limits, nor from any lot without said fire limits, to any lot within said fire limits, nor from any part of any lot within said fire limits to any other part of the same lot. (*As Amended by Ordinance Approved Jan.* 16, 1866.)

To prohibit repairing wooden buildings when more than half its value is destroyed by fire.

SEC. 5. When any wooden building within the fire limits shall be partially destroyed by fire or otherwise, and the damage thereto shall not exceed the half of its value, at the time of such partial destruction to be ascertained in the manner hereinafter provided, such building may be repaired and not otherwise.

Permission to build or repair wooden buildings partially destroyed by fire.

SEC. 6. In case of the partial destruction by fire or otherwise of any wooden building in said fire limits, it shall be the duty of the Marshal and the owner of such building, to proceed at once to choose each one a disinterested and competent builder to estimate the value of such building at the time of such partial destruction, the amount of damages thereto, and if the persons so choosen cannot agree, then they shall call in a third disinterested builder, and the estimate of any two of them shall be binding on the City as well as on the owner of such building. If the amount of the damages exceed that provided in Section five, the Marshal shall give a written permit to such owner, to repair his building, and shall also keep a record of the same in his office. *Provided*, that the value spoken of shall be construed to mean the cash price for which such building can be put in the same condition as it was at the time of the disaster.

Regulation as to including.

SEC. 7. On the application in writing of the owner or owners of the greater part of the ground of any block not included within the fire limits, the Common Council may by resolution extend to such block the provisions of this Ordinance relating to the erection, repair and removal of buildings within such limits.

Publication.

SEC. 8. Every such resolution shall be published for two successive weeks in the official newspaper of the City.

SEC. 9. For each and every week which a building erected, placed, removed or repaired, contrary to the provisions of this Ordinance, shall be allowed to remain, the owner of such building may be complained of as for a distinct offence and punished as hereinafter provided. Every week a distinct offense.

SEC 10. No person shall without permission of the Common Council, use or occupy within the limits of the City of East Saginaw, any building for storing powder, or for the manufacture of turpentine, camphene, lime or other dangerous or easily inflamable or explosive substance. To prohibit the manufactury of turpentine, etc.

SEC. 11. No person shall in this City have, put or keep any hay or straw in stacks or piles without having the same securely enclosed, so as to protect it from flying sparks of fire. Hay and straw to be secured.

SEC. 12. All carpenters and others, making or using shavings shall at the close of each day, cause the same to be securely stowed in some safe place remote from danger by fire. [*As Amended by Ordinance Approved June* 16, 1866. To secure shavings.

SEC. 13. No lighted candle, or lamp, shall be used in any stable, building or other place where hay, straw, hemp, flax, rushes, shavings, gunpowder or other combustible materials shall be stowed, or lodged, unless the same is well secured in a lantern. To secure lights.

SEC. 14. Every chimney hereafter built, or erected, shall be so constructed as to admit of being scraped, brushed, or cleansed. Constructi'n of chimneys.

SEC. 15. No pipe of any stove, or chimney shall be put up or used, unless the same be conducted into a chimney made of brick or stone, nor shall any such pipe be put up so as to project through the chimney into the open air, and in all cases where a stovepipe passes through the woodwork of a building, it shall be separated from such woodwork, at least six inches by sheet iron or other incombustible material. Method of putting up stove pipes.

SEC. 16. Every chimney or stove pipe in use in this City, shall be swept, scraped or burnt out, in every three months, and if burnt out, the same shall be done on a wet or rainy day, or when the roof is covered with snow. Chimneys and stove pipes to be swept and cleaned, and when done.

SEC. 17. No person shall carry any fire in or through any street, alley or lot in this City, unless the same be placed in some covered pan or vessel. Not to carry fire unsecured.

Not to deposit ashes unless secured in proper vessels or ash houses.

SEC. 18. No ashes shall be kept or deposited in any part of this City, unless the same be kept or deposited in a close iron or earthern vessel, or brick or stone ash house, thoroughly secured.

Not to kindle fires in any street, alley or lane in the thickly populated portion of the city.

SEC. 19. No person shall kindle any fire or furnish the materials for any fire, or in any way authorize any fire to be made or kindled in any street, alley or vacant place within the thickly populated portions of this City.

To regulate the use of fire arms, fire works, etc.

SEC. 20. No person shall fire, or set off any squib, cracker, gun powder, or fireworks, or fire any cannon, gun or pistol in any street, lane or alley, or in any yard, public or private unless by a written permission from the Mayor, and such permission shall specify the object and limit the time of such firing. This Section shall not be extended to the prohibition of the usual demonstration on the 4th of July and the 22d of February.

Provisions for scuttle and stairway.

SEC. 21. Every building, more than one story in height, shall have a scuttle through the roof and a convenient stairway leading to the same.

To regulate the storing of gun powder.

SEC. 22. There shall not be kept in any house, or its appurtenances within the fire limits of this City, except in a magazine, to be approved of by the Marshal, at any one time, more than twenty-eight pounds of gunpowder, which shall be secured in metal cannisters, with metal stoppers or covers, and no one canister shall contain more than seven pounds. Any gunpowder kept contrary to this Section, shall be seized by the Marshal, and on conviction before the Recorder's Court of the party so keeping the same, it shall be forfeited to the use and benefit of the City, to be sold under the direction of the Mayor, and the offender shall be punished as hereinafter provided.

To regulate the carrying of gunpowder through the streets.

SEC 23. Persons carrying gunpowder through the City, to or from the Magazine, shall secure the casks in which the same is contained by good canvass, tow cloth or leathern bags.

The Marshal's duty to inquire and investigate as to the safe condition of buildings.

SEC. 24. The Marshal shall have the right and power, and it is hereby his duty, at such times as he may deem it necessary, between sunrise and sunset, to enter any and all buildings and enclosures, to discover whether the same are in a dangerous state, and if they are, to cause such to be put in a safe condition, he shall also have the power, and it is hereby made his duty to see that all chimneys, hearths, fire-places, fire-arches, ovens, stove-pipes, kettles, boilers or any structure or apparatus that may be dangerous in causing or promoting fires, are constructed in such a manner as to secure the greatest protection against fire. He shall also have power, and it is hereby made his duty, to require of the owner or occupant of any blacksmith shop, furnace or fundry, to erect, alter or reconstruct his chimney, so as to prevent sparks from passing into the open air. Every person who shall neglect for forty-eight hours after he is notified in writing, or otherwise, by the Marshal, to comply with the requirements provided herein shall be punished as hereinafter provided.

Regulation as to propellers and steamboats.

SEC. 25. No steamboat or propeller shall land or haul along side of any wharf, dock or bank within this City or nearer than one hundred feet of any such wharf, dock or bank, unless said boat or propeller have a good and sufficient spark catcher covering the smoke pipe of such boat or propeller so as to prevent any sparks passing from the fires of said boats into the open air to the danger of fire of any property in said City. In case of violation of the provisions of this Section, the master, owner or person having charge of said steamboat, propeller or other craft, shall be fined upon conviction thereof in the Recorder's Court, a sum not less than fifty dollars and not exceeding five hundred dollars, and shall also in the discretion of the court, be imprisoned in the City prison or county jail not exceeding ninety days.

Who liable when offence is committed by minors or servants, etc.

SEC. 26. If any offence shall be committed against this Ordinance, or by any child, apprentice or servant, the forfeiture and penalty prescribed in this Ordinance, shall be recovered from and paid by the parent, master or mistress of the party so offending.

Duty of Marshal and Constables to make complaint.

SEC. 27. It shall be the duty of the Marshal and Constables of the City, to make complaint for any violation of the provisions of this Ordinance, and their neglect or refusal to do so, shall be sufficient cause for their removal from office.

Penalty.

SEC. 28. Any violation or failure to comply with any of the provisions or requirements of this Ordinance, except as specified in Section 25, shall be punished by a fine not exceeding one hundred dollars, and in the imposition of any such fine, the court may make a further sentence that the offender, on failing to pay the penalty imposed be imprisoned in the City prison or county jail, of Saginaw county, for any term not exceeding ninety days. [*As Amended by Ordinance Approved October* 19, *A. D.* 1863.

FOR THE EXTENSION OF THE FIRE LIMITS.

Block 68, included within the City limits.

That block 68, of Hoyt's Plat is hereby included within the fire limits of the City of East Saginaw, and the provisions of all Ordinances of a general nature relating to the fire limits shall be applicable and extend to said block 68. [*As Amended November* 19, 1866.]

CHAPTER XLIV.

OF STEAM FIRE ENGINE COMPANIES.

[Ordinance Approved April 11th, 1867].

The Common Council may by resolution establish a Steam Fire Engine Company.

SECTION 1. Whenever in the opinion of the Common Council it is necessary to establish a Steam Fire Engine Company, it shall so declare by resolution.

Each Company shall consist of a foreman, etc.

SEC. 2. Each Company shall consist of a Foreman, an Engineer, two Drivers, five Hose Men and one Fireman, to be appointed by the Common Council, on the recommendation of the Mayor and Chairman of the Committee on Fire Department, and to hold their office during good behaviour.

Salaries.

SEC. 3. The officers and men shall receive the following annual salaries payable monthly. The Foreman, one hundred dollars: the Engineer, one thousand dollars; the Engine Driver, seven hundred and thirty dollars; the Hose Cart Driver, Fireman and Hosemen each fifty dollars.

Duties of the Foreman on an alarm of fire.

SEC. 4. On an alarm of fire, the Foreman shall immediately with his Engine and Company repair to the scene of the same, and under the direction of the Chief or Assistant Engineer of the Fire Department get his engine into service and remain with his Company as long as his services are required; he shall preserve order in his Company going to, at the fire, coming from the same and at all times when out with his Company for exercise, duty or parade.

Duties of the Engineer.

SEC. 5. The Engineer shall be *ex-officio*, Secretary of the Company, shall record in a legible hand in a book to be provided by the City for the purpose, the name, age, time of admission and discharge of each member of the Company, he shall keep an accurate account and be held strictly responsible for all public property in charge of the Company, and note the absence of members from fires on the last day of each month and oftener if required: he shall make a written report to the Controller, setting forth the names of the members of the Company, the number of times each of them has been absent from fires and the condition of the Engine, apparatus and other property in charge of the Company; he shall see that the engine house and stable are kept clean and that the Engine Driver keeps the horses and harness in good condition and that the engine, hose cart, hose and horses are always ready for instant service, and that proper order is preserved in and about the engine house.

Specifications of the duties of Engineer, Engine driver and hose cart driver.

SEC. 6. The Engineer and Engine Driver shall be at all times at or in the immediate vicinity of their engine house, except when absent on duty, and shall devote their entire time and attention to the duties of their office; at night the Hose Cart Driver shall sleep in the engine house and always be ready to perform his duties as Hose Cart Driver; the Engineer, Fireman and Driver shall accompany their engine to all fires and under the direction of the Foreman discharge their respective duties; the Engineer shall be a practical mechanic and engineer, and shall see that the engine is kept clean and always ready for instant service.

Duties of Engine driver.

SEC. 7. The Engine Driver shall have the care and charge of the horses and harness and keep the same in good condition, repair and ready for instant service. He shall be under the direction of the Engineer and shall assist him in taking care of the horse, and in the performance of all necessary work in and about said engine house.

Duties of hosemen.

SEC. 8. The Hosemen, on an alarm of fire, shall immediately repair to the scene of the same, report themselves to the foreman and perform such duties as shall be required of them.

Conditions necessary to retain a person in said Company.

SEC. 9. No person shall be accepted or retained in said Company, whose place of business and lodging is not within four blocks of their engine house, and who cannot upon all ordinary occasions perform their duties as members of said Steam Fire Engine Company, and in case of sickness or other unavoidable cause for absence, all members shall have previously furnished a good and acceptable substitute and have reported the same in writing to the Engineer, who shall also in writing report the same to the Controller.

To furnish a substitute and make a report of the same.

To prohibit the use of spirituous liquors or intoxication in or about the Engine house.

SEC. 10. No spirituous liquors shall be allowed in the engine house or stable, and any member bringing such liquor in any such stable or engine house, or who shall be intoxicated in or about the same, or at any time shall upon complaint and satisfactory evidence thereof be discharged by the Mayor. Any member against whom charges may be preferred to the Mayor, may by him be suspended from duty and pay until such charges are disposed of.

To prohibit tippling, rioting or immoral conduct in or about the Engine house.

SEC. 11. No person shall tipple, riot or be guilty of any lewd, lucivious or disorderly conduct in or about any steam fire engine house. Complaints for a violation of any of the provisions of this Ordinance shall be made in writing by the Engineer of the Company to the Controller, who shall investigate the same and report in writing with his opinion to the Mayor, who is hereby authorized to remove any member for cause.

Penalty.

SEC. 12. Officers and men absent from a fire without a good excuse and contrary to the provisions of this Ordinance shall be fined as follows: The Foreman, five dollars; the Engineer, twenty-five dollars; the Engine Driver, ten dollars; The Fireman, Hose Cart Driver and Hosemen, each two dollars, to be deducted from their pay at the end of the month.

SEC. 13. All Ordinances heretofore approved relative to Steam Fire Engine Companies are hereby repealed.

SEC. 14. This Ordinance shall take immediate effect.

CHAPTER XLV.

OF PAID HAND ENGINE COMPANIES.

[Ordinance Approved October 31st, 1870.]

SECTION 1. Whenever in the opinion of the Common Council, it is necessary to organize a Paid Hand Engine Company, it shall so declare by resolution. Common Council may establish paid hand EngineCompanies.

SEC. 2. Each Company shall consist of a Foreman and a Steward and twelve men, to be appointed by the Common Council on the recommendation of the Mayor and the Chairman of the Committee of Fire Department, and to hold their office during good behavior. Who shall constitute a paid hand EngineCompany.

SEC. 3. No person shall be a member of any such company who is under twenty-one or over forty-five years of age, and who does not reside within a quarter of a mile of the place where his engine is located. Qualifications for membership

SEC. 4. The Foreman and Steward shall each receive an annual salary of one hundred dollars, and the men an annual salary of fifty dollars each, the same to be paid quarterly. Salaries.

SEC. 5 On an alarm of fire, they shall immediately repair to their engine house, and with the engine and apparatus proceed to the scene of the fire, and through their Foreman report to the Chief or Assistant Engineer, whose order they shall obey. Companies to repair to fires on an alarm thereof.

SEC 6. The Foreman shall be Secretary and perform the following duties: He shall record in a legible hand in a book, to be provided by the Controller, the name, age, time of admission and discharge of each member. He shall keep an account of all public property in charge of the Company. He shall call the roll after each alarm and note the absentees, and when the engine has been in service, the roll shall be called before the Company starts for home, and the absentees noted. He shall once in each month, and oftener if required, make a report in writing to the Chief Engineer of the Fire Department in which he shall give the names of the members, the number of times each has been absent from roll call and the cause therefor, and the condition of the engine, hose cart, hose and other public property in charge of the Company. He shall cause the engine house, engine and all Duties of the Foreman.

apparatus connected therewith, to be kept clean and ready for service. He shall be responsible for the behavior of his men when on duty. He shall have the command of his company and the control of all public property which his company may have in charge and shall also assign to each man the duty he is to perform at fires and in taking care of the engine and apparatus.

Members may be removed for cause. SEC. 7. If any member of the company refuses or neglects to perform any duty assigned him by the Foreman, or is guilty of any disorderly or improper conduct, he may on complaint, be removed from office by the Mayor.

Companies may make rules. SEC. 8. The Company may make rules for its own government not inconsistent with this Ordinance, subject to the approval of the Common Council.

Supplies to be furnished by Controller. SEC. 9. All needful supplies for the Company shall be furnished by the Controller, upon the written order of the Foreman.

Duties of Steward. SEC 10. The Steward shall keep the engine, hose and hose cart in good running and working order, and shall be assisted from time to time by the members of the Company, who shall be regularly detailed for that service.

Penalties for absence from fires. SEC. 11. Any Foreman or Steward who is absent from roll call without a good excuse, shall forfeit for each absence the sum of two dollars, to be deducted from his pay at the end of each quarter, and each member who is absent from roll call without a good excuse, shall forfeit for each absence the sum of one dollar, to be deducted from his pay at the end of each quarter. It shall be the duty of the Foreman or acting Foreman, at the end of each quarter, to make a full and accurate report (verified by his affidavit) to the Controller, and the Controller shall make his pay-roll therefrom.

Assistant Foreman to be elected. SEC. 12. The Company shall elect an Assistant, who, in the absence of the Foreman, shall perform his duties.

Foreman to have powers of Policemen. SEC. 13. The Foreman shall possess and exercise the powers and duties of a Policeman without pay from the City, for the preservation of the peace at fires and in and about his engine house.

No tippling, &c., allowed. SEC. 14. No person shall play a card, tipple, riot or be guilty of any lewd or lascivious conduct in or about any engine house.

SEC. 15. On the complaint in writing of any other members of a Company against the Foreman thereof, it shall be the duty of the Mayor to investigate the charges preferred and report the evidence with his opinion thereon to the Common Council. Disorderly conduct in the Engine house prohibited.

SEC. 16. The Officers and Men of the Paid Hand Engine Companies may be removed at any time by the Mayor or Common Council. Officers and men may be removed.

SEC. 17. In going to and returning from fires, the members of Companies shall make as little noise as possible, and where there are paved streets shall not use the sidewalks. Noises in streets prohibited.

CHAPTER XLVI.

OF PAID HOOK AND LADDER COMPANIES.

[Ordinance Approved October 31st, 1870.]

SECTION 1. Whenever in the opinion of the Common Council, it is necessary to organize a Hook and Ladder Company, it shall so declare by resolution. Common Council may establish Hook and Ladder Companies by resolution.

SEC. 2. Each Company shall consist of a Foreman, a Steersman and six Hook and Ladder men, to be appointed by the Common Council on the recommendation of the Mayor and the Chairman of the Committee on Fire Department, and to hold their office during good behavior. Who shall constitute a paid Hook and Ladder Company.

SEC. 3. No person shall be a member of any such Company who in under twenty-one or over forty-five years of age. Qualificati'n of membership.

SEC. 4. The following annual salaries shall be paid: The Foreman, two hundred and fifty dollars; the Steersman, two hundred and fifty dollars; The Hook and Ladder men, each one hundred dollars. The said salaries shall be paid monthly. Salaries.

SEC. 5. The Foreman shall be the Secretary of his Company and keep its books and records. He shall record in a legible hand in a book, to be provided by the Controller, the name, age, time of admission and discharge of each member. On the breaking out of a fire, he shall at once proceed with his Company to the scene of the same and aid in its extinguishment under the orders of the Chief or Assistant Engineer. He shall record the absence of any member from duty and at the end of each month report to Duties of Foreman.

the Controller, giving an account of all public property under his control, its condition, the names of the members absent from each fire, and the number of times they were so absent with their excuses.

Duties of Steersman.

SEC. 6. The Steersman shall act under the direction of the Foreman, and shall keep his truck and truck house in good order.

Companies to repair to fires on an alarm thereof.

SEC. 7. On an alarm of fire, the members shall repair at once to the truck house and report to the Foreman for duty.

Penalties for absence from duty.

SEC. 8. Any Foreman or Steersman who is absent from any fire without good cause, shall forfeit the sum of three dollars, to be deducted from his pay at the end of each month.

Foreman to make report to Controller.

SEC. 9. The Foreman shall make report at the end of each quarter, to the City Controller, giving the names of the members of his Company, and the number of times each has been absent from roll call, and their excuse therefor, and the Controller shall make his pay roll therefrom.

Companies may make rules.

SEC. 10. Each Company may make rules for its own government, not inconsistant with this Ordinance, subject to the approval of the Common Council.

Assistant Foreman to be elected.

SEC. 11. The Company shall elect an Assistant, who, in the absence of the Foreman shall perform his duties.

Foreman to have powers of Policeman

SEC. 12. The Foreman shall possess and exercise the powers and duties of a Policeman for the preservation of the peace at fires, and in and about his truck house.

Disorderly conduct prohibited.

SEC. 13. No person shall playat cards, tipple, riot, or be guilty of any lewd or lascivious conduct in or about any truck house.

Mayor, etc., to investigate charges against Foreman.

SEC. 14. On the complaint in writing of any member of the Hook and Ladder Company against the Foreman, the Mayor and Chairman on the Committee on Fire Department, shall investigate the charges contained in such complaint, and report to the Common Council with their opinion thereon.

Officers and men may be removed.

SEC. 15. The officers and members of any Hook and Ladder Company may be removed at any time by the Mayor or Common Council.

Noises in streets prohibited.

SEC. 16. In going to and returning from fires, the members of Hook and Ladder Companies shall make as little noise as possible, and where there are paved streets shall not use the sidewalks.

TITLE IX.

OF RESTRAINING ANIMALS.

CHAPTER XLVII.

OF POUNDS AND POUND MASTERS.

[Ordinance Approved November 7th, 1870.]

SECTION 1. The Marshal, when directed by the Common Council, shall construct one or more good and suitable pounds, at such place or places in said City as shall be designated for such purpose by said Common Council, to be placed under the care and direction of a pound keeper for each pound in said City, to be appointed by the Common Council, who shall act as such pound keeper during the pleasure of such Common Council

Marshal to contract and Council to direct where built.

SEC. 2. Before entering upon the duties of his office, the Pound Master shall execute a bond to the City of East Saginaw, in the penal sum of five hundred dollars with two sureties, for the faithful performance of the duties of his office, and shall also subscribe the oath of office prescribed by Section 25, Title 2, City Charter. The bond and oath shall be filed in the office of the City Clerk.

Bond and oath.

SEC. 3. Hereafter no swine, sheep, horses, mares, asses, mules, neat cattle, goats or geese shall be permitted to run at large within the limits of said City, and if found running at large within the limits aforesaid, each and every one of said animals may be impounded in the common pound of said City, whence they shall

Horses, swine, etc., shall not run at large except, etc.

not be released until the owner or owners, or some person in his, her or their employ shall pay to the Pound Keeper his fees and charges, for the sustenance thereof, as hereinafter provided; and the owner or owners of such animal, upon conviction of permitting any such animal to run at large, shall be subject to pay a fine not exceeding five dollars, in the discretion of the court, and the costs of prosecution for every such offence: *Provided, however*, that nothing in this Ordinance shall be construed so as to prevent milch cows from running at large during the day from five o'clock in the morning until nine o'clock in the evening, from April 1st to December 1st; and in the night time from six o'clock in the evening until seven o'clock in the morning, from December 1st to April 1st.

No minor to take up etc., except authorized.

SEC. 4. It shall not be lawful for any minor, unless authorized by a Pound Keeper or by written certificate signed by the parent or guardian of such minor, directed to the Pound Keeper to take up, distrain or impound any such animal as aforesaid, within said pound limits, and no Pound Keeper shall impound any such animal or animals as aforesaid, taken up or distrained by any minor, except as above stated.

Pound master to feed animals.

SEC 5. The Pound Master shall receive, keep and feed any animal or fowl which may be brought to the pound.

Pound master to keep record.

SEC. 6. The Pound Master shall record in a book, to be kept for that purpose, and which shall at all times be open for public inspection, the time when any animal or fowl was received. He shall also keep a record of all sales, and the amount for which each animal and fowl was sold.

Sale of impounded animals.

SEC. 7. The Pound Master shall on Saturday of each week, at the public pound, sell at public auction any horse, ass, ox or cow, which has been impounded therein for a period of six days, and all other animals and fowls which have been impounded therein for a period of three days, and are unclaimed, or whose owners refuse to pay the fees hereinafter provided. Notice of such sale shall be given three days prior thereto, and shall contain a description as near as may be of the animals or fowl to be sold, and shall be posted in three conspicuous places in the City, one of which shall be the Post Office, and shall also publish said notice in one of the Daily Newspapers in East Saginaw, at least once before said date of sale.

SEC. 8. The proceeds arising from the sale of any animal or fowl, shall after deducting all lawful fees and costs on Saturday of each week be paid into the City Treasury, and shall constitute a separate fund to be disposed of as provided in Section 9.

Proceeds of sales to be paid into the City Treasury.

SEC. 9. The monies arising from said sale and paid into the Treasury, as provided in the last section, shall be delivered to the former owner of such animal or fowl, on satisfactory proof to the Treasurer, that he or she was the owner. *Provided*, that all monies deposited as aforesaid which may remain unclaimed for the period of one year, shall be transferred and credited by the Treasurer to the sinking fund.

Surplus to be paid to owners of animals.

SEC. 10. The Pound Master shall on Saturday of each week report under oath in writing to the City Controller, giving a detailed statement of the animals and fowls impounded since their last report; the number of animals and fowls claimed and sold, and the amount of money received by reason of fees and sales, and the quantity of hay and grain used for the pound, and the amouut paid into the City Treasury since their last report; and in case he should fail to file such statement, he shall forfeit and pay a fine of not less than five dollars nor more than twenty-five dollars in the discretion of the court.

Pound Master to make report.

SEC. 11. The Pound Keeper shall be entitled to exact and receive the following fees: For receiving and discharging any of the animals to wit: Horses, asses, neat cattle and swine the sum of one dollar each and no more, and fifty cents a day for keeping. For receiving and dischargiug any of the following animals, to wit: Sheep, goats and geese the sum af twenty cents each and no more, and twenty-five cents a day for keeping. Also, in case any animal impounded is advertised for sale as provided in Section four of said Ordinance, they shall be entitled to exact and receive for each notice of sale so posted respectively as aforesaid, the sum of twenty cents, and the legal fees for advertising; also in case of the sale of any animal impounded, they shall be entitled to exact and receive for such sale five per cent. of the gross proceeds of

Fees of the Pound Master.

such sale, but the City shall in no case be liable to the Pound Keeper for any part of the pay and charges mentioned in this and the following sections.

Resistance to persons taking up animals prohibited. SEC. 12. No person shall hinder, delay or interfere with any one who is driving or carrying any animal or fowl to the Public Pound.

Breaking into pounds prohibited. SEC. 13. No person shall break or attempt to break or assist in breaking into any Public Pound.

Pound Keepers to have power of Policeman. SEC. 14. Pound Keepers shall possess and exercise the powers and duties of Policemen for the preservation of the public peace, the property of the City, and all animals impounded by them.

Illegal impounding prohibited. SEC. 15. No person shall take up, drive or carry to the Public Pound any animal or fowl not legally liable to be impounded therein.

Pound Keeper not to be interested. SEC. 16. No Pound Keeper shall be directly or indirectly interested in the purchase of any animal sold by him under the provisions of this Ordinance.

Penalty. SEC. 17. Any violation of the provisions of this Ordinance shall be punished by a fine not to exceed one hundred dollars and costs, and in the imposition of any fine and costs, the court may make a further sentence that the offender be committed to the county jail or city prison until the payment thereof for any period not exceeding thirty days.

SEC. 18. An Ordinance, entitled "An Ordinance concerning Pounds and certain animals impounded," made and passed the 11th day of March, A. D. 1867, and all amendments thereto are hereby repealed.

CHAPTER XLVIII.

OF DOGS.

[Ordinance Approved June 13th, 1870.]

Tax on dogs. SECTION 1. Upon each dog in this City, a tax of two dollars per annum shall be paid by its owner or possessor, to be livied and collected in the same manner as other City taxes upon personal property.

SEC. 2. The owner or possessor of any dog shall put around the neck of the same, a collar, upon which shall be engraved or marked the name of the owner or possessor. Collars to be placed on dogs.

SEC. 3. Any person who shall suffer to be or remain in or about the premises occupied by him or her, or to run at large, any dog not having a collar thereon, as required by section two of this Ordinance, may be punished as hereinafter provided. Dogs not to run at large without collars.

SEC 4. Any dog found at large, not having a collar thereon, as herein required, may be impounded as hereinafter provided. Dogs without collars may be impounded.

SEC. 5. It shall be the duty of the Marshal, Assistant Marshal, Constables, and such person or persons as may be authorized by the Common Council; and it shall be lawful for any person to take up and impound any dog found at large, between the first day of May and the first day of October, without a good and sufficient muzzle, rendering it impossible for such dog to bite. Who shall take up and impound dogs without collars.

SEC. 6. The Common Council shall provide a suitable place to be used as a Dog Pound, in which all dogs found running at large, contrary to the provisions of this Ordinance, shall be impounded; such pound shall be provided with a suitable vat or basin in which all dogs unclaimed, as provided in next section, shall be drowned. Dog Pound.

SEC. 7. At the setting of the sun on each day, all dogs which have been twenty-four hours impounded under the provisions of this Ordinance, and unclaimed, shall be drowned, and their bodies buried by the City Scavenger at the expense of the City. Unclaimed dogs to be drowned.

SEC. 8. The Pound Master of the pound, where the dog ground is located, shall have charge and control of the same, and the owner may reclaim any dog impounded, on paying the said Pound Master for the benefit of the City, the sum of one dollar. Pound Master to have control of Dog Pound.

SEC. 9. The Pound Master shall on Saturday of each, week pay into the City treasury, all moneys by him received under this Ordinance; and shall at the same time report, under oath, to the City Treasurer, the number of dogs impounded since his last report, the number redeemed, the number drowned and the amount of fees received; and the Treasurer shall at the time of the making of said report, pay to the said Pound Master three-fourths of the money received by him, at the time of making said report, as the Pound Master's fees for his services. Pound Master to make report and pay over moneys.

Vicious dogs to be muzzled.

SEC. 10. If any owner or possessor of a fierce or vicious dog shall permit the same to run at large without being provided with a good and sufficient muzzle, rendering it impossible for such dog to bite, he or she shall be punished as hereinafter provided.

Female dogs shall not run at large.

SEC. 11. Any owner or possessor of a female dog, who shall allow the same to run at large while in heat, shall be punished as hereinafter provided, and it shall be the duty of the Marshal and his Assistants to cause any female dog so running at large to be slain.

Penalty.

SEC. 12. Any person violating or failing to comply with the provisions of this Ordinance, shall be punished by a fine not to exceed one hundred dollars and costs, and in the imposition of any such fine and costs, the court may make a further sentence, that the offender be imprisoned in the City prison or county jail upon the payment thereof, not exceeding thirty days.

SEC. 13. The Ordinance entitled "An Ordinance relative to Dogs," made and passed July 11, 1859, is hereby repealed.

TITLE X.

OF HACKS, DRAYS AND PORTERS.

CHAPTER XLIX.

OF STANDS FOR DRAYS.

[Ordinance Approved July 26th, 1869.]

SECTION 1. No drays, or other vehicles, used as a public dray, while not in actual use for draying purposes, shall stand upon any public street of said City, unless the owner or driver thereof first obtains permission in writing from the owner or occupant of the building or premises in front of which such dray or other vehicle shall stand. *Provided*, That such permission given to stand in front of any building or premises may at any time be revoked by the owner or occupant thereof by twenty-four hours notice in writing served on the owner or driver of such dray or vehicle. [*As Amended by Ordinance March* 20, 1871.] Streets upon which they are to stand.

SEC. 2. Each Drayman who shall violate the provisions of the preceeding section of this Ordinance, shall on conviction thereof pay a fine not exceeding one dollar and costs for each offence. Penalty.

CHAPTER L.

OF DRAYS.

[Ordinance Approved April 11th, 1859.]

Drays, etc., to be licensed. SECTION 1. That no person or persons shall engage or become interested in the business of carting, conveying, transporting or carrying property of any description whatever for hire or reward within the corporate limits of said City, with any cart, wagon, sleigh or any other vehicle, without first having obtained a license from the Common Council of said City, authorizing him or them to carry on such business or to be engaged or interested therein, except when transporting for themselves or for said City.

Conditions of license, etc. SEC. 2. No person or persons shall receive such license until he or they shall have paid to the Treasurer of said City three dollars for each and every horse and cart, or sleigh, or other vehicle, or six dollars for each pair of horses and wagon, or sleigh or other vehicle, or other team and vehicle, nor until the Marshal of said City shall have filed with the Clerk thereof his certificate that such person or persons applying for the same has a good and sufficient horse or horses, dray or drays, wagon or wagons, sleigh or sleighs, and other necessary things and facilities for carrying on such business.

Carts or vehicles to be marked. SEC. 3. The Clerk of said City upon the production of the City Treasurer's receipt for the amount fixed by Section two of this Ordinance for such license, and upon filing with him of the Marshal's certificate as aforesaid, shall issue such license signed by the Mayor and by said Clerk under the corporate seal of said City, and thereupon shall register in a book provided for that purpose, the name of the person or persons so licensed and the number thereof in the order in which granted, time of granting, time when the same expiees, the amount paid therefor. And the person receiving such license shall thereupon cause his or their names and the number of said license to be painted in large figures on both sides of each cart or vehicle or other conspicuous place thereon.

Compensation for drayage. SEC. 4. Hereafter each and every person or persons engaged with carts, drays or other vehicles using one horse plying or carrying property for hire within the limits of the City of East Saginaw shall be entitled to receive, demand and collect for each load carried, the following rates, to-wit: Two blocks distance and under, twenty-five cents; and two blocks distance and under four blocks, thirty-five cents; over three quarters of a mile, fifty cents; over three quarters of a mile and to extent of City limits, seventy-five cents and no more. And each and every person so employed with two horses and vehicles, shall be entitled to receive fifteen cents in addition to foregoing rates. [*As Amended by Ordinance approved August* 1, 1864.]

SEC. 5. All carts, drays, wagons or other vehicles licensed as aforesaid with the person in charge thereof and engaged in transporting property in said City for hire, shall while waiting for employment, occupy the following streets, and no other, that is to say: On either side of German street unobstructed, so as not to interfere with or to oppose the ingress to or egress from any of the buildings on said street situate; every person driving and in charge of any such cart, dray, wagon or other vehicle, shall wear on his hat or cap a badge with the word "Carman" painted thereon in letters not less than one half inch in diameter and the number of license of the vehicle of which he has charge, also painted thereon of a larger size. [*As Amended by Ordinance Approved May* 7, *A. D.* 1860.] Stands for drays, etc. Carmen to wear badge on cap.

SEC. 6. Carmen shall be required to dray or cart any article required upon the payment of the proper fee at any time from six o'clock in the morning to eight o'clock in the evening. Draymen shall not refuse employment.

SEC. 7. Any person violating or offending against any of the provisions of this Ordinance, shall be liable to pay on conviction thereof before the Recorder of said City or any Justice of the Peace thereof, a fine of not less than three dollars, nor more than twenty-five dollars, and in default of payment thereof shall be imprisoned in the City prison not less than one nor more than twenty-five days. Penalty.

CHAPTER LI.

OF PORTERS AND RUNNERS.

[Ordinance Approved Feb. 15, 1869.]

Mayor to issue license to Porter, etc.

SECTION 1. The Mayor of the City of East Saginaw for the time being shall have power from time to time, to issue licenses under his hand and seal to so many and to such persons as he shall think proper to carry on the business of Public Porters and Runners for hotels, and to all Omnibus Agents, Omnibus Drivers and Carriers of Baggage, and all other persons when acting as Porters and Runners for hotels. The Mayor or the Common Council shall have power to revoke any and all of such licenses.

When expire.

SEC. 2. All such licenses shall expire on the first day of May next after the date thereof, and may be renewed on application of the holders thereof.

Amount to be paid.

SEC. 3. For every such license shall be paid by the person applying for the same, the sum of one dollar, and for every renewal the same sum.

No person to act as such without license.

SEC. 4. No person shall act or engage in the business of Public Porter or Runner for any hotel, or as an Omnibus Agent, Omnibus Driver or any person acting as Porter or Runner for hotels without being duly licensed by the Mayor, under the penalty not exceeding five dollars, in the discretion of the court and costs of prosecution for each offence.

To wear a badge.

SEC. 5. Every Public Porter or Runner, Omnibus Agent, Omnibus Driver, and every person acting as a Runner for hotels, shall wear a badge on his hat or in a conspicuous place on his body, on which shall be legibly and plainly engraved or printed his name and the number of his license under a penalty not to exceed five dollars, in the discretion of the court and the costs of prosecution, for each neglect of the provisions of this Section.

Acts which are forbidden.

SEC. 6. No Porter, Runner, Trackman, Drayman, City Expressman, Omnibus Agent, Omnibus Driver, Carrier of baggage or other persons acting as Porters or Runners for hotels, so licensed as aforesaid, shall on the arrival of any steamboat or rail road cars in the City of East Saginaw for a period of fifteen minutes thereafter, go upon or approach within twenty feet of the wharf or depot, where such steamboat or rail road cars have made fast or stopped running, or are about to make fast or stop running unless such Porter, Runner, Hackman, Drayman, City Expressman, Omnibus Agent, Omnibus Driver or Carrier of Baggage be requested to move some trunk or other baggage from said wharf or depot, in which case it shall be lawful to go near, in or upon such steamboat or depot for such purpose, under a penalty not to exceed five dollars, in the discretion of the court, and costs of prosecution for every such offence. Penalty.

SEC. 7. On conviction of any Porter, Runner, Omnibus Agent, Omnibus Driver or Baggage Carrier, or other persons acting as Porter or Runuer for any hotel or public house, licensed as aforesaid before the Recorder's Court of any violation of the provisions of this Ordinance, the Mayor or Recorder shall in his discretion be authorized in addition to the fine hereinbefore provided to vacate, and annul any such license that may be held by any such Porter, Runner, Omnibus Agent, Omnibus Driver or Carrier of Baggage. May forfeit license in addition.

SEC. 8. No such Porter, Runner, Omnibus Agent, Omnibus Driver or Carrier of Baggage shall be entitled to charge to exceed the sum of twenty-five cents for carrying a passenger and ordinary baggage any distance within the present City limits and for any charge in excess to the above, shall be liable, on conviction to pay a fine not to exceed five dollars and costs of prosecution for each offence. Their charges.

TITLE XI.

OF PLACES OF AMUSEMENT AND RECREATION.

CHAPTER LII.

OF BALL ALLEYS, BILLIARD TABLES, &C.

[Ordinance Approved July 11th, 1859.]

Power of Common Council to grant license

SECTION 1. No person shall keep or permit to be kept in or about any premises occupied by him, her or them, within the limits of said City, any ball alley, or any billiard table or other tables, for the purpose of playing at any game for hire, gain or reward whatever, or to allow any person or persons to play at such alley or such table or tables, unless the person keeping the same has been previously licensed to do so by the authority of the Common Council of said City.

Application for license and its time to run.

SEC. 2. It shall be the duty of any person or persons who may be desirous of keeping any ball alley, billiard table or other table, to make application to the Common Council of said City for license, and such license may be granted on paying the sum and on filing the bond hereinafter required; but no such license shall be granted for a shorter period than three months nor to exceed one year.

Bond.

SEC. 3. No person shall receive such license until he shall have paid to the Treasurer of said City, such sum as the Common Council may determine for each and every ball alley, billiard table or other tables. The person applying for any such license shall also enter into a bond to the Common Council of said City in the sum of five hundred dollars with sufficient securities to be approved by the Common Council of said City, conditioned that such applicant shall well and truly keep all the requirements of this Ordinance, and shall neither do nor permit to be done anything contrary thereto.

To restrain gaming, rioting, betting, etc., and keeping open on Sabbath.

SEC. 4. No person licensed as aforesaid shall at any time permit or suffer any gaming for money or other value within any ball alley or billiard room or other such establishment kept by him, nor shall any person be guilty of betting, or gaming for money or other value therein, nor shall any person so licensed suffer therein or thereabouts any drunkeness, quarrelling, fighting or any other disorderly conduct, nor keep any such establishment open during any part of the Sabbath, or first day of the week, or after the hour of eleven o'clock in the evening, or before the hour of seven o'clock in the forenoon of any day, nor permit to stay thereon or thereat, any minor or apprentice after the parent or guardian of such person shall have notified such keeper not to permit such minors or apprentices to play.

Penalty.

SEC. 5. Any person or persons who shall offend against the provisions of this Ordinance, shall on conviction thereof, be liable to a fine not exceeding one hundred dollars and costs of prosecution for each offence, and on conviction the person so licensed shall be liable to have his license suppressed and annulled. *Provided*, That the Common Council may at any time, on proof sufficient being made to them of a violation of any of the provisions of this Ordinance revoke and annull such license.

CHAPTER LIII.

OF GAMING.

[Ordinance Approved September 12th, 1870.]

Fraudulent gaming prohibited.

SECTION 1. No person shall manage, use or practice any game, or device whatever, with intent to cheat or defraud another.

Gaming in hotels and streets, etc. prohibited.

SEC. 2 No person shall play for money or other valuable thing, with cards, dice, tables, wheels of fortine, machines, billiards, nine or ten pins, or other instruments or devices whatever, in any hotel, grocery, eating or victualing house, store, boat, shop, tavern saloon, beer hall, bar-room or other public or private building, in any highway, street, lane, alley, public space or square or elsewhere within the City of East Saginaw.

Renting buildings for gaming prohibited.

SEC. 3. No person shall let or rent any building to be used for gaming purposes.

Keeping buildings or instruments for gaming prohibited.

SEC. 4. No person shall keep any building, instrument or means for gaming.

Instruments for gaming to be destroyed.

SEC. 5. Any instrument kept for the purpose of gaming, for money or other valuable thing, shall be destroyed by the Marshal or any Policeman of the City, under the direction of the Chief of Police, and the neglect or refusal to obey such an order, shall be deemed sufficient cause for removal from office.

Lotteries prohibited.

SEC. 6. No person shall keep, maintain, direct or manage, or aid in the keeping, maintaining, directing or managing any lottery for the drawing or disposing of money, or any other property whatever.

Penalty.

SEC. 7. Any violation of or failure to comply with the provisions of this Ordinance, shall be punished by a fine not exceeding one hundred dollars and costs; and in the imposition of any such fine and costs, the court may make a further sentence, that in default of the payment thereof, within a time to be fixed in such sentence, the offender shall be committed to the City prison or county jail for a period of time not exceeding thirty days.

CHAPTER LIV.

OF SHOWS AND PUBLIC EXHIBITIONS.

[Ordinance Approved March 2d, 1858.]

To license shows, etc.

SECTION 1. That no person or persons within said City shall act, exhibit, play or perform any play, farce, show, opera or other theatrical performance, circus riding or feats of horsemanship, menagerie or exhibition of animals, panorama, diorama, painting, sculpture, natural curiosity, tricks of legerdemain, musical party, concert, or any other exhibition, entertainment, show or amusement of whatever name or nature, for which money or any other reward is in any manner demanded or received, without a license or permit for that purpose first had from the Mayor or acting Mayor, and in his absence from the City Clerk; which license shall express to whom and for what it is granted, and the time it is to continue.

SEC. 2. That neither the Mayor or City Clerk shall deliver such license or permit to any person or persons, until he or they shall have paid to the City Treasurer, (who shall give a receipt for the same, to be filed in the office of the City Clerk,) the following sums, to wit: For any theatrical exhibition or opera, five dollars for each day or twenty dollars for each and every week of performance.—For circus, riding or feats of horsemanship, or for menageries of animals, the sum of thirty-five dollars per day. For any musical concert, panorama, diorama, exhibition of statuaary or paintings, or any natural curiosity, in halls or buildings, two dollars per day; and for the like class under canvass or a side show for circuses and menageries, each five dollars per day. For all other exhibitions or performances for gain, three dollars per day or ten dollars per week. *Provided*, That for lectures upon scientific, historical or literary subjects or for exhibitions or fairs given or made by citizens or associations of this City, no license or permit shall be required. To regulate the price of such licenses

SEC. 3. That the Common Council may by a majority vote of its members, grant a yearly license to any public hall, and in case such annual license be granted, no additional license shall be required of any theatrical troupe or concert exhibiting therein. *Provided*, This section shall not be construed to do away with the permit as required in case of other exhibitions. Yearly license.

SEC. 4. That no person shall act, exhibit, show or perform in or cause to be acted, exhibited, shown or performed, or be in any manner concerned in the acting, exhibition, showing or performances of any indecent or blasphemous play, farce, opera, public exhibition, show or entertainment, or performance of any kind, whatever, nor shall any permit be given to play, show or exhibit upon the Sabbath. To prohibit indecent and blasphemous plays, and all plays upon the Sabbath.

SEC. 5. That no person shall sell, give or distribute by lottery or by any scheme of chance, any personal or real property, to or To prohibit lottery or any scheme of chance.

among any person or persons attending, or proposing to attend any exhibition or performance mentioned in this Ordinance.

Penalty. SEC. 6. That any person offending against any of the provisions of this Ordinance shall be liable to pay a fine of not less than twenty-five nor more than one hundred dollars for every such offense, and the Marshal of the City of East Saginaw is hereby authorized, and it is made his duty to arrest or cause to be arrested any person or persons offending against the same, and bring him or them before the Recorder's Court, or any Justice of the Peace of said City, who shall thereupon proceed to hear, try and determine the same. *Provided*, That such person or persons may be discharged by the Mayor or any three Aldermen, upon paying such sum, not less than the required license, as they may direct, and costs.

SEC. 7. All Ordinances or parts of Ordinances heretofore passed, which conflicts with the provisions of this Ordinance, are hereby repealed.

TITLE XII.

OF DRAINS AND SEWERS.

CHAPTER LV.

OF BOARD OF SEWER COMMISSIONERS.

[Ordinance Approved June 19th, 1866.]

SECTION 1. There shall be appointed in the month of June, 1866, three Sewer Commissioners, who shall hold their offices for the term of one, two and three years respectively, and the term for which each one is appointed shall be designated in the resolution of appointment, and in the month of April, each year thereafter, there shall be appointed one Sewer Commissioner to hold his office for three years, who shall each qualify as in the charter prescribed. Time of appointment and term of office.

SEC. 2. The said Commissioners shall as soon after their appointment in each year, as practicable organize as a Board by the election of a President shall appoint subject to the approval of the Common Council, a Sewer Engineer, who may be the City Surveyor and the Sewer Engineer shall act as Secretary of the Board, and shall under the direction of the Board keep the records and the papers of the Board, superintend the construction and repairs of all public sewers or drains built by special assessment or out of any public monies voted or raised for that purpose. The salary or pay of the Commissioners and the Sewer Engineer shall be such as the Common Council shall by resolution determine. Organization.

Record of acts and doings.

SEC. 3. Said Board shall keep full and exact records of all their doings, which shall always be subject to the inspection and direction of the Common Council, and shall have the supervision of the construction of all sewers hereafter to be built, whether built at the expense of the City or by special assessment, upon the property to be benefitted thereby, and of all repairs of sewers and pools hereafter to be made and are hereby fully authorized and empowered to enforce or otherwise carry out all contracts for the building or repairing of sewers, drains and pools within said City.

To submit a place for the construction of sewers and drains for the whole City, together with a report of the probable expense thereof.

SEC. 4. Said Board shall as soon as may be, submit to the Common Council a plan for constructing sewers and drains for the whole City, and such as should be constructed this year, and shall in the month of April in each year, report to the Common Council what public sewers and drains they deem necessary to build in that year, and shall accompany the report with an estimate of the cost of each and all said sewers and drains and all the probable expenses of the construction of public sewers during the year next ensuing.

To advertise for proposals to build the sewers and drains ordered to be built by the Common Council.

SEC. 5. The Common Council shall decide what public sewers and drains shall be built and whether by general tax or by special assessment on the owners or occupants of the property to be benefitted thereby, and shall through the City Clerk notify the Board of their decision, and said Board shall without delay report to said Common Council an estimate of the cost of any sewer or drain which the Common Council shall thus order to be built, and which was not embraced in the estimate provided for in the foregoing section, and shall proceed to advertise for proposals to build the sewers and drains ordered to be built by the Common Council, under such specifications and forms as the Board shall deem necessary; which advertisement shall be published at least ten days in the newspaper contracted with to do the City printing and shall state the time and place when and where said proposals shall be received, and shall require each party making a proposal to accompany the same with a statement in writing signed by at least two persons who agree thereby to become sureties in an amount at least double the estimated cost of the work proposed to be performed for the faithful performance of said work. Said proposals shall be received and opened by said Board publicly in the office of the City Controller, and in his presence, and a copy of each proposal shall be recorded by said Controller and also by the Secretary of the Board.

SEC. 6. When said proposals shall have been received and opened as aforesaid, said Board together with the Controller shall examine the same and determine who are the lowest responsible biddders possessing the necessary qualifications, and the Controller shall forthwith communicate such determinations together with all said proposals to the Common Council, who shall consider the same and award the contract proposed to be performed to the lowest responsible bidder, and shall return said proposal and communicate their decision to said Board. The said Board shall transmit the proper specifications of the work to be performed to the City Attorney, who shall draw the necessary contract for the work in accordance with such specifications, which contract shall be signed on the part of the City by said Board and attested under the corporate seal of the City Clerk, and shall when executed, be placed in the keeping of said Board, whose duty it shall be to see that the contractor or contractors comply therewith.

Method of accepting proposals. Drawing of and signing contract with the lowest responsible qualified bidder.

SEC. 7 All the proceedings for building sewers and drains and pools by special assessment, shall be under the provisions of the Charter so far as this Ordinance is inconsistent with the Charter.

Proceedings for building sewers and drains to be under the provisions of the charter.

SEC. 8. Said Board shall certify to the amount due upon all contracts and for all materials furnished and labor performed in building or repairing sewers, drains or pools, and all bills and accounts thus certified for amounts so due shall be audited by the Controller and presented by him to the Common Council in the same manner as other bills and accounts against said City.

To certify to expense of building sewers, etc.

SEC. 9. Said Board shall at the first regular meeting of the Common Council in the month of March in each year or oftener if required, submit to said Common Council a report of all their proceedings with the names of their employees and the total expenses of the construction and repairs of sewers, drains and pools since the last report, and such other information as they may deem necessary or as said Council may require.

Time to report on the construction and repairs of sewers, drains, etc.

Duty to repair sewers and drains in case of unexpected casualty and the amount allowed for such repairs.

SEC. 10. Said Board shall not lay down or construct any sewer, drain or pool in said City, or purchase any materials, or enter into any contract except as provided in this Ordinance, and except in case of any unexpected casualty or damage to the sewers, pools or drains of said City, in which case said Board may cause the same to be repaired to the amount of not exceeding five hundred dollars, and shall report their proceedings therein and the necessity therefor to the next regular meeting of the Common Council.

Penalty.

SEC. 11. No connection shall be made with any public sewer or drain, except with the permission of said Board and under the direction of the Sewer Engineer, who shall at least once in each month notify the City Assessor of all such connections made since the last notice, and any person connecting with any public sewer or drain without such permission, and any person injuring any such sewer or drain shall be fined not to exceed one hundred dollars or imprisoned not to exceed three months, or both, in the discretion of the court.

Stationary.

SEC. 12. The City Clerk shall supply the said Board with all necessary stationary.

CHAPTER LVI.

OF PUBLIC AND PRIVATE DRAINS AND SEWERS.

[Ordinance Approved October 24th, 1870.]

No lot to be drained without application to the Common Council or Board of Sewer Commissioners, and paying of assessments.

SECTION 1. No person or persons shall be permitted to connect any drain from his, her or their premises, with any public drain or sewer, now made or constructed, in said City, nor with any private drain whereby his, her or their premises will be drained into any public drain or sewer, except on previous application in writing to and permission by the Common Council or Board of Sewer Commissioners, and the payment of the assessment hereinafter mentioned.

Board of Sewer Commissioner to determine size of drain to be entered under supervision of Engineer.

SEC. 2. All private drains to be hereafter made by individuals in any public street, lane or alley in said City, and connected with any public drain or sewer, shall be of such size, dimensions and materials, and constructed and laid as directed by the Board of

Sewer Commissioners, and shall enter such public drain or sewer under and according to the personal supervision and direction of their Engineer; nor shall any person or persons enter any public drain or sewer at any other places than those designated and fixed for that purpose in the construction thereof.

SEC. 3. The amount which individuals using or being benefited by any public drain or sewer, shall pay for such use, is hereby fixed as follows: The sum of one dollar and fifty cents annually for each cellar drained by box, directly or indirectly into any public drain or sewer, which assessment shall be taken to include all other drainage of the premises to which said cellar especially belongs; and the sum of fifty cents annually for each lot or subdivision of lot, being without a cellar drained by box as aforesaid into any public drain or sewer, and such sums as may be fixed by the Board of Sewer Commissioners for all establishments requiring an unusual or extraordinary amount of drainage, drained as aforesaid upon actual inspection of and report thereon by the Assessor. Assessment for draining cellars.

SEC. 4 Said assessment shall in all instances be paid when the City and school taxes are collected. When to be paid.

SEC. 5. Any person whose premises are drained directly or indirectly into any public drain or sewer, or any person using said premises thus drained, or for whose benefit or family the same be used, shall be liable to the payment therefor, and in addition said assessment shall become and be a charge and lien on the premises thus drained and be recovered, and the same proceedings had in every respect for the recovery thereof, as are provided for the recovery of other special assessments; and the corporation may also, at their option, stop such private drain, and prevent any person from draining his premises into any public drain or sewer, where such assessment shall not be paid in advance on the second application, and said privilege shall not be restored unless on the payment of the tax and a forfeit, or of double the amount of the assessment. Persons using drain or sewer liable to assessment. Assessment liens on lots, how collected.

SEC. 6. Any person who shall remove any grate from the pool over which it is placed, or in any way directly or indirectly injure any public drain or sewer, or any part thereof, shall on con- Penalty for injuring drains.

viction thereof, before the Recorder's Court, be liable to a penalty for each offense not exceeding one hundred dollars and costs.

Penalty for constructing drains without permission.

How to enter drains.

SEC. 7. Any person who shall connect any drain from his premises into any private drain which enters into any public drain or sewer, without first making the application, procuring the permission and paying the assessment provided for in the first section of this Ordinance, shall on conviction of each offense before the Recorder's Court be liable to a penalty not exceeding one hundred dollars and costs; and any such person who shall construct and lay any private drain, connecting with any public drain or sewer, or who shall enter any public drain or sewer in any other manner except as is provided for in the second section of this Ordinance shall be liable for each offence on like conviction, to a penalty not exceeding one hundred dollars and costs; and any person who shall enter any public drain or sewer at any other place than is designated and fixed for that purpose in the construction thereof, shall be also liable to pay for each offense on like conviction, a penalty not exceeding one hundred dollars and costs; and if any person shall drain his premises along the side of any public drain or sewer, he shall also be liable to pay a penalty not exceeding one hundred dollars and costs on like conviction. *Provided*, That this section shall not be construed to extend to any case where a private drain has heretofore been laid down along the side of any public drain or sewer, but such private drain shall not be repaired by any person without having received from the Board of Sewer Commissioners or some authorized officer of the City, a certificate that such repair will not endanger the safety and preservation of any public drain or sewer along the side thereof.

Drain not to be placed by public drain.

When sewers may be entered.

SEC. 8. No person shall be permitted to connect any drain from his premises with the main sewer, nor enter the same between the first day of December and the first day of April in each year, and any person offending against this section, shall on conviction of such offense before the Recorder's Court be liable to pay a fine of one hundred dollars and costs.

What drains are public.

SEC. 9. All drains now made and constructed, or which shall hereafter be made and constructed by the corporation, shall be deemed to be public drains or sewers within the provisions of this Ordinance; and all moneys received under the provisions of this Ordinance, shall be stated and kept in a separate account are all hereby specially pledged and appropriated to the following use and objects and no other, to wit: *First*, To defray the expense of indispensable repairs of existing sewers. *Second*, To defray the cost of additional public sewers and their repairs. *Third*, To apply on the interest of the City debt, accruing on account of the costs of constructing and maintainance of such sewers.

How sewer assessments to be appropriated.

SEC. 10. The assessment provided for in this Ordinance shall be collected in the manner prescribed by the Ordinance relating to the collection of special assessments, the provisions of which are made applicable hereto, except that the time for the warrants and the provisions of per centage shall be made to correspond with the terms of the warrants and the provisions for the per centage in the collection of the City and School taxes

How sewer assessments may be collected.

SEC. 11. No person shall be permitted to connect any drain from his, her or their premises with any drain or sewer made by one or more individuals in any street, lane or alley as aforesaid, unless on payment to the proprietors of such drain or sewer of a rateable proportion of the expense of making the same, the amount to be ascertained and determined by the Board of Sewer Commissioners with the right to appeal to the Common Council, nor shall any person make or construct a sink, drain or sewer, leading into any other drain or sewer without putting a sufficient strainer at the head of it, under a penalty not exceeding ten dollars and costs for each offense.

Certain portions of expense to be paid before connecting with drains.

SEC. 12. Every person having any drain from his, her or their premises, that shall hereafter be made as aforesaid, shall pay a rateable proportion of all expenses necessary for maintaining and keeping such drains or sewers in repair, such proportion to be ascertained and determined in the manner provided for in the foregoing section; and if any person shall neglect to pay the same when so ascertained, such person shall forfeit and pay the sum of two dollars and costs for each week during which the same shall remain unpaid.

How expense of repairing ascertained.

Penalty.

Marshal to notify persons to repair.

SEC. 13. In all cases where drains or sewers shall be obstructed so as to become in the opinion of the Board of Sewer Commissioners a nuisance, it shall be their duty to give notice to the persons using the same to repair such drains or sewers and if the same be not forthwith repaired, it shall be the duty of the Board of Sewer Commissioners to cause the necessary repairs to be made and to charge the said persons with a rateable proportion of the expense, incurred including a reasonable allowance to the Commissioners for their own services, subject to the appeal to the Common Council, as is provided in the tenth section; and all such appeals shall be made within the time in which such person is required to pay the sums above required, and if any person shall refuse or neglect to pay their proportion of the charges for the space of ten days after notice, he or they shall be liable upon conviction before a court of competent jurisdiction, to pay a fine not exceeding fifty dollars and costs of suit.

No connection to be made until Surveyor shall have ascertained the grade.

SEC. 14. No connection with public or private sewers or drains shall be made under the provisions of this Ordinance, until the City Surveyor shall have designated the grade therefor, under the penalty of twenty dollars.

CHAPTER LVII.

OF FILLING LOW GROUNDS.

[Ordinance Approved July 25th, 1870.]

Certain lots to be filled when notice is given.

SECTION 1. All lots lying between Washington street on the West, and Jefferson street on the East, and between the German Colony Road on the South, and Johnson street on the North, and which or any part of which are below the grade of Franklin and Cass streets, as established by this Council, shall be filled by their owners respectively to a height within eighteen inches of the grade of said streets; such filling to be done with saw dust or earth or other material approved by the Street Commissioner, and which shall prevent the arising of noisome effluvia from such low lots and grounds; such filling to be done by such owners respectively within forty days after a service on them of a printed copy of this Ordinance.

SEC. 2. It shall be the duty of the Marshal to give notice in writing to such owner, occupant or proprietor personally, or by leaving the same at his place of residence in said City, requiring him to comply with said order, a copy of which shall be annexed to said notice, and the Marshal shall make due return or report to the Common Council of his doings in the premises. *Provided*, That if such person cannot be found or has no place of residence in said City, the Marshal shall cause notice to be published three weeks in some newspaper in said City, unless the Common Council shall otherwise order, and an affidavit of the publication of said order shall be filed with the Clerk of the City. Duty of the Marshal in such cases.

SEC. 3. As the filling of low lots is ordered as a sanitary measure, it is further ordained that each owner of a lot or lots, who shall neglect or refuse to fill the same herein ordered, within the time prescribed, shall be liable to and shall pay a fine of one dollar for each day beyond the time designated, which any owner by him shall remain unfilled as aforesaid. The refusal or neglect to fill punished

SEC. 4. In case any owner or owners of lots shall neglect to fill the same within the time prescribed, the Common Council shall cause the same to be filled, and the expense thereof shall be paid to the City, by such owner on demand, and the same shall be a lien on the lot or lots so filled, until the same shall be paid, and payment may be enforced by an action of debt therefor, or by an assessment and sale of the premises under the provisions of the Charter for such purposes. Common Council to order lots filled in certain cases.

SEC. 5. An Ordinance entiled "An Ordinance to provide for the filling of certain low grounds, be and the same is hereby repealed.

TITLE XIII.

MISCELLANEOUS.

CHAPTER LVIII.

ORDINANCE GRANTING PERMISSION TO CERTAIN PERSONS TO ESTABLISH AND LOCATE STREET RAILWAYS.

[Ordinance Approved October 19th, 1863.]

Preamble. WHEREAS, William L. P. Little, William J. Bartow, William Gallagher and Moses B. Hess, all of East Saginaw, Michigan, except William Gallagher, who is a resident of Salina, Mich , and William J. Bartow, who is a resident of the City of East Saginaw, Michigan, their associates, successors and assigns, propose to organize as a body politic and corporate under an Act entitled "An Act to provide for the construction of Street Railways," approved February 13th, 1855, and the acts amendatory thereto for the purpose of constructing and opening Street Railways in and through the streets of the City of East Saginaw. Therefore be it ordained by the Common Council of the City of East Saginaw:

Consent, permission, etc. granted and given to W. L. P. Little and others to lay a Street Railway in the City of East Saginaw. SEC. 1. That consent, permission and authority are hereby exclusively given, granted and only vested in the said William L. P. Little, William J. Bartow, William Gallagher and Moses B. Hess, their associates, successors and assigns, to lay a single or double track for a Railway with all necessary and convenient tracks for turnouts, side tracks and switches in and along the course of the streets and bridges in the City of East Saginaw, and the same to keep, maintain and use and to operate thereon Railway Cars and Carriages during all the term hereinafter specified and prescribed, and in the manner and upon the conditions set forth in the Ordinance; and that said grantees, their successors, associates or assigns, shall not be required to construct any such Railway through any of said streets or bridges in any one year, except a Railway on Washington street in said City, extending from the present depot of the Flint and Pere Marquette Railway to Bristol street, which shall be constructed within eighteen months from the first day of January, 1864, and also a Railway on said Washington street from Bristol street to the south line of said City, which shall be constructed within two years from the first day of January, 1864.

Time limited to construct.

The rate of fare for any distance not beyond Bristol street, in either direction, shall not exceed five cents for each passenger, in any one car, and shall not exceed ten cents for any point beyond Bristol street in any one car.

Fair.

SEC. 2. The Railways through all the streets shall be laid in the center thereof, if of a single track, and, if of a double track, the rails of each track shall be laid within two feet and four inches of the center of the street, and said rails shall be laid four feet eight inches apart so as to accommodate the most common width of carriage wheels. When the grantees shall complete one track of the said Railway and place cars thereon for the public use, they may at any time thereafter build a second track. *Provided*, They do not interrupt the running of their cars on the first completed track.

Conditions of laying track, etc.

SEC. 3. The track of said Railway shall be laid in such manner as shall least obstruct the free passage of vehicles and carriages of the same, and the rails shall be laid flush with the surface of the streets, and shall conform to the grade thereof as now established, or as they shall from time to time be established or altered. The grantees, or their assigns shall be required to keep the surface of the streets inside of the rails and for two feet four inches outside thereof in good order and repair, and all dirt and filth cleaned and removed therefrom as the Common Council may from time to time direct.

Manner of laying track.

Animals to be used.

SEC. 4. The cars to be used on said Railways shall be drawn by animals and at a speed not exceeding the rate of six miles per hour, and shall be run as often as public convenience shall require, and the Common Council shall prescribe. *Provided*, That said Council will not require them to run oftener than once in twenty minutes during fourteen hours every day, from the 15th of April to the 15th of October and twelve hours every day from the 15th of October to the 15th of April, and the cars in use upon said Railways shall be run for no other purpose than to transport passengers and their ordinary baggage and freight, and the cars and carriages for that purpose shall be of the best style in use on such Railways in other cities.

Time of running only such speed.

To regulate the carrying of baggage.

SEC. 5. Each passenger shall be allowed to take free of charge such ordinary baggage as he can carry in his hands, and not take up more room than he is entitled to for his seat. The grantees, or their assigns, may charge such price for carrying any baggage, as may be just and proper. *Provided*, That in no case shall more than five cents be charged for carrying a trunk or other ordinary baggage, such as usually carried free on steamboats or railroads worked by steam.

To avoid collisions and accidents.

SEC. 6. Cars driven in the same direction shall not approach each other within a distance of three hundred feet, except in cases of accident or at stations, or for the purpose of connecting two cars together.

Cars not to stop on the crosswalks, etc.

SEC. 7. No cars shall be allowed to stop on a cross walk. nor in front of any intersecting street, except to avoid collisions, or prevent danger to persons in the streets.

Provision for stopping at the intersection of streets.

SEC. 8. When the Conductor of any car is requested to stop at the intersection of streets, to receive or leave passengers, the cars shall be stopped so as to leave the rear platform slightly over the crossing.

Character of men employed.

SEC. 9. The grantees or their assigns shall employ careful, sober and prudent agents, conductors and drivers, to take charge of their cars while on the road, who shall use every precaution not to do an injury to a team, carriage or person on foot.

Conductors not to allow ladies or children to leave car while in motion.

SEC. 10. Conductors shall not allow ladies or children to enter or leave the cars while on motion.

SEC. 11. The cars shall at all times be entitled to the track, and any vehicle upon the track of said Railways shall turn out when the cars come up so as to leave the track unobstructed, and the drivers of any vehicle refusing to do so shall be liable to a penalty not exceeding five dollars on conviction before the Recorder's Court, of said City of East Saginaw, and costs of prosecution.

Right of cars to track.

Penalty.

SEC. 12. The car, after sunset, shall be provided with signal lights.

Signal lights

SEC. 13. Nothing in this Ordinance shall be so construed as to prevent the Common Council authorizing the laying down of water and gas pipes and sewers, or repairing the same, and the grantees shall have no claim for damages against said City Gas or Water Companies. *Provided*, The work of laying down said water or gas pipes and sewers, shall be done in such a manner as not unreasonably to damage or injure said Railway or their use.

Not to prevent laying down gas pipes, etc.

SEC. 14. If said grantees or their assigns shall fail to complete the aforesaid Railway according to the conditions prescribed by this Ordinance, then the rights and privileges granted shall be forfeited, together with any and all improvements made upon the said Railways, to the City of East Saginaw, unless the Common Council of said City shall give to the said grantees a further extension of time. *Provided*, If said grantees shall be delayed by the order or injunction of any court. *Provided*, Said injunction is not obtained by reason of the consent or convenience of the said grantees. *Provided* That if the said grantees shall use diligence to have the injunction removed, then the time of such delay shall be excluded from the time of completion prescribed by the requirements of this Ordinance.

Forfeiture.

Provisions.

SEC. 15. The Common Council reserve the right to make such further rules, orders or regulations as may be deemed necessary to protect the interests and accommodation of the public in relation to said Railways.

Reservation of rights by Common Council.

SEC. 16. The powers and privileges, proposed to be conferred by the provisions of this Ordinance, shall be limited to thirty years from and after the date of its passage.

Time limited.

Ordinance.

SEC. 17. The Ordinance shall be void and of no effect, unless the grantees shall within two months from the date of this Ordinance notify the Common Council in writing of their acceptance of and agreement to the provisions of this Ordinance.

CHAPTER LIX.

ORDINANCE PROVIDING FOR THE ESTABLISHING GAS WORKS TO THE CITY OF EAST SAGINAW

[Ordinance Approved April 20th, 1863.]

Who are authorized and permitted to use streets, etc., for the purpose of laying down gas pipes.

SECTION 1. That Thomas Edsall, James L. Ketcham, Hiram A. Jones, John F. Driggs and Julius K. Rose, their associates, successors and assigns, be, and they are hereby authorized and permitted to use the streets, lanes, alleys and public grounds of said City, with the streets, lanes, alleys and public grounds within all territory that may be hereafter added to the said City for the purpose of laying down, under and through said streets, lanes, alleys and public grounds, pipes for conveying gas for supplying said City and the inhabitants thereof, with gas lights, and for the repairing of the same pipes. *Provided*, That said gas pipes shall not interfere with the necessary construction of sewers for the drainage of said City, and that Thomas Edsall and others above named, their associates, successors and assigns, shall give one days notice to the Superintendent of Streets or other proper authority, previous to the opening of any street, lane, alley or public ground, and shall obey all reasonable directions of said Superintendent of Streets, or other proper authority, as to guarding all excavations and openings made in laying or repairing their said pipes, so as to prevent all accidents to persons or property, and shall, within a reasonable time, close and repair such streets, lanes, alleys and public grounds, as they may have opened, leaving them in as good condition as they were previous thereto, and keep the same in good repair from the effect of such digging or taking up.

Gas pipes not to interfere with the construction of sewers, etc.

Notice to be given to the Superintendent of streets.

Streets, etc., to be left in as good condition as they were before opened.

SEC. 2. That in consideration of the privilege aforesaid, the said Thomas Edsall, and others above named, their associates, successors and assigns, shall furnish to the said City and its inhabitants upon such streets, lanes, alleys and public grounds (in and through which the leading or main pipes may be laid), such quantity of gas as may be required at the average rate paid by neighboring Cities of like population, and similarily situated as to the cost of manufacturing Gas and not to exceed four dollars for each one thousand cubic feet (lamp posts, meters and fittings for public lamps to be furnished by or at the expense of the City) and that said Thomas Edsall, James L. Ketcham, Hiram A. Jones, John F. Driggs and Julius K. Rose, their associates, successors and assigns, shall on or before the first day of December, 1863, commence the erection of works for the manufacture of Gas, and shall progress with the same in such manner as to ensure their completion by the first day of December, 1864, together with the laying of one and one-quarter miles of leading or main pipe, said pipe to be of cast iron or other substance equally as good for the purpose, and all the work for the manufacturing of Gas and the pipes, fixtures and meters, to be constructed in the most approved and substantial manner. *As Amended by Ordinance approved Sept. 22, 1863.*]

To furnish gas at average rates paid by neighboring cities, and not to exceed $4 for each M cubic ft.

Lamp posts, etc., to be furnished by the City.

Time to commence and complete the erection of Gas Works.

SEC. 3. Said Thomas Edsall, James L. Ketcham, Hiram A. Jones, John F. Driggs and Julius K. Rose, their associates, successors and assigns, shall, within sixty days after the passage of this Ordinance, organize under the Act of the Legislature of the State of Michigan, entitled "An Act to authorize the formation of Gas Light Companies," approved February 12, 1855, and file their acceptance of this Ordinance and a copy of their Articles of Association with the City Clerk, and shall within the same time deposit with the City Treasurer the sum of one thousand dollars to be by him kept as security for their compliance with this Ordinance, and, if they, their associates, successors or assigns shall fail to comply with this section, or shall fail to comply with section two of this Ordinance, as regards the time of commencing and completing the said works and laying of pipes as therein stated, then and in that case said sum of one thousand dollars and all rights and privileges conferred by this Ordinance shall be deemed forfeited, and said deposit shall be paid into the City Treasury, to

To organize and file their acceptance of this Ordinance. Also a copy of articles of association with the City Clerk.

One Thousand Dollars security.

Forfeiture.

To repay deposit. the credit of such fund as the City shall direct, and in case of the commencement and completion of said works at the time and in the manner as aforesaid deposit shall be repaid.

Privileges granted after fulfilling conditions. SEC. 4. That in case said Thomas Edsall, James L. Ketcham, Hiram A. Jones, John F. Driggs and Julius K. Rose, their associates, assessors and assigns, fulfill all the conditions of this Ordinance, they shall have the exclusive privilege of laying pipes for the conveyance of Gas in and through the streets, lanes, alleys and public grounds, and beneath the sidewalks to the stores, dwellings, public offices and other buildings in said City, for the term of thirty years from the passage of this Ordinance. *Provided*, That if they shall not comply with the conditions mentioned in section three of this Ordinance, or shall at any time fail for a term of three months to keep the said Gas Works, pipes, meters and fixtures in good order, or to furnish the City or the inhabitants to the requisite quantity of Gas as was supplied at the commencement of said term, this Ordinance and all the rights, benefits and privileges thereby conferred shall be deemed forfeited and said Common Council may confer said rights, benefits and privileges upon any other persons, association or corporation. But nothing in this act shall be construed to prevent or prohibit the cutting off or refusing the usual supply of Gas from or to any person or persons on account of any neglect or refusal to pay for the same.

What forfeited if Sec. 3 is not complied with.

May alter or amend this Ordinance. SEC. 5. The Common Council of said City may at any time alter or amend this Ordinance so as to regulate the manner of laying the pipes and the opening and closing of the streets, lanes, alleys and public grounds, of the City, not inconsistent with the rights granted under this Ordinance, and may by resolution or Ordinance passed between the first day of May and the first day of August in every fifth year, establish, regulate and change the price which shall be charged the City and individuals for Gas under this Ordinance, which resolution or Ordinance shall be in force and binding upon all concerned for five years, and until altered, except their said proposed Company may make such prices less. *Provided*, That the price to be charged for Gas as established by said proposed Gas Company, shall not be changed by the Common Council until after the expiration of ten years from the passage of this Ordinance. ***And Provided further,*** That the price for which such is to be furnished shall not be made lower then the price charged for Gas in other cities of this State similarly situated with reference to the cost of manufacturing the same.

CHAPTER LX

ORDINANCE RELATIVE TO ENFORCING THE ORDINANCES OF THE CITY.

[Ordinance Approved July 11th, 1859.]

SECTION 1. In all cases where a fine or penalty is imposed or may hereafter be imposed by any Ordinance of this City, such fine or penalty may be sued for and recovered in the Recorder's Court, in the name of the City. *Provided,* This Ordinance shall not be construed to divest Justices of the jurisdiction given by the Charter or Ordinance of the City. Recorder and Justice Court.

SEC. 2. The Recorder's Court shall have power to hear and determine, in a summary manner, all charges for violating any of the Ordinances of the City, and for that purpose may issue a capias as commencement of suit, or, in case the offender is brought before the said court without process, may proceed to hear and determine the case without any writ or for such violation, suit may be commenced by filing declaration or by writ of summons in the usual form. Recorder's Court Jurisdiction.

SEC. 3. All Police Justices of this City shall have concurrent jurisdiction with said Recorder's Court, to hear and determine all charges for violating any Ordinance of said City, when the greatest penalty thereof shall not exceed one hundred dollars fine or ninety days imprisonment, and such fine or penalty may be sewed for and recovered in said Justice's Court. [*New Section Approved by Ordinance passed July* 22, 1861.] Police Justice's Jurisdiction.

CHAPTER LXI.

PROVIDING FOR THE PUNISHMENT OF CERTAIN CRIMES AND OFFENSES BY HARD LABOR

[Ordinance Approved April 13th, 1868].

Punishme't of crimes by hard labor. SECTION 1. That any male person over the age of sixteen years who shall be convicted of the offense of vagrancy, obsceuity, indecent and lascivious behaviour, intoxicating, gaming, gambling, disorderly conduct, keeping disorderly house, keeping or visiting a house of ill fame, disturbance, riot or breach of the peace, in violation of any Ordinance of the City, in case of imprisonment upon such conviction shall, in the discretion of the court be liable to labor during the term of such imprisonment upon the public streets of the City in cleaning or otherwise improving the same. Such labor shall be performed in the charge of any Police Officer or any officer, appointed by the Mayor, and under the direction of the Street Commissioner.

Time of labor. SEC. 2. Every person who shall be sentenced to imprisonment to hard labor, as provided by Section one of this Ordinance, shall labor ten hours of each day, (except Sundays) during the term of his imprisonment, and shall perform all such reasonable labor in shoveling, cleaning or othewise improving the public streets, as shall be required, and when not thus employed at labor, shall be confined in the City prison or jail; and it shall be unlawful for any person sentenced to imprisonment and labor, to refuse to perform such labor when required, or to escape from such labor: and if any person sentenced to labor as aforesaid, shall escape, the Chief of Police or any Police officer may re-arrest such person, and the term of imprisonment to labor of such person shall continue from the time of his re-arrest the same as though he had not escaped.

Duty of the Chief of Police to enforce this Ordinance. SEC. 3. It is hereby made the duty of the Chief of Police, when any person or persons shall be sentenced to imprisonment to hard labor, as provideded by this Ordinance, to cause such person or persons to perform such labor and in such manner as shall be directed by the Street Commissioner; and if any person or persons liable to imprisonment and labor, shall have escaped from such labor, or shall refuse to perform the labor required, the Chief of Police is hereby authorized to attach to such person a suitable ball and chain sufficient to ensure such labor or prevent escape, and it is hereby made the duty of the Street Commissioner to direct all labor which shall be performed by virtue of this Ordinance.

CHAPTER LXII.

OF POSTING ADVERTISEMENTS.

[Ordinance Approved October 28th, 1867.]

SECTION 1. No person shall stick or post any handbill or placard of any description upon any public or private building or upon any post, fence, bill board or any other structure or thing whatever, the property of another, without the permission of the owner or occupant of the same. To prohibit posting bills without permission.

SEC. 2. Any person violating the provisions of this Ordinance, shall be fined a sum not exceeding twenty-five dollars, and in default of the payment of such fine, shall be imprisoned in the county jail of Saginaw county or in the City prison for a term not exceeding thirty days, in the discretion of the court. Penalty.

CHAPTER LXIII.

OF THE DIVISION AND EXPENDING OF THE HIGHWAY FUND.

[Ordinance Approved July 1st, 1867.]

SECTION 1. It shall be the duty of the Controller of the City of East Saginaw, to open an account with each of the wards of said City, and to credit to each ward such sum or sums, as may from time to time be levied by order of the Common Council for highway purposes within the ward, which funds shall be known and designated as the "First Ward Highway Fund" the "Second Controller to open accou't with each of the Wards of the City.

Ward Highway Fund" and the "Third Ward Highway Fund." Upon the completion of any assessment roll in which a highway fund is levied, the Controller shall certify to the Common Council the amount of highway fund placed to the credit of each ward, which certificate shall be filed with the City Clerk and be printed in the proceedings of the Common Council.

City Treasurer also to open an account with said Wards.

SEC. 2. The City Treasurer shall in like manner open an account with the serveral wards, and shall keep the highway to each separately, and pay the same out only on orders drawn upon the said ward highway fund and shall report monthly the balance due on said fund as required by law in regard to other funds

Marshal to separate the funds collected for Highway purposes.

SEC. 3. The Marshal, in the collection of tax rolls shall separate the funds collected for highway purposes, and shall certify to the City Treasurer the amounts collected upon the property of each ward, as near as may be, and shall take receipts therefor, and file the same with the City Clerk as provided by law.

Funds to be expended for the repair of streets, etc., and special provisions.

SEC. 4. The several ward funds created and separated by this Ordinance shall be expended only for the repairs of streets, lanes and alleys of the several wards as shall from time to time be directed or authorized by the Common Council. *Provided*, That no such repairs shall be made until the same shall be recommended by a majority of the aldermen elected for such ward. And whenever application shall be made for the repair of any street, by any number of feeholders of said City, it shall be the duty of the Alderman elected for said ward, within one week to examine said street and to report to the Common Council at its next meeting the necessity of such repairs, and the amount as near as may be required to put the same in good condition. After the making of such report, the Council may authorize the expenditure of such sum, as it may deem necessary to repair said street, not exceeding the amount recommended therefor by the Alderman of the ward. In case any street to be repaired shall be upon the boundary line of any ward and partly within two wards, the Aldermen of such wards shall act jointly in recommending such appropriations and repairs.

Moneys to be expended under direction of Street Commissioner and special provisions.

SEC. 5. All moneys thus appropriated to repair streets shall be expended by and under the direction of the Street Commissioner as ordered by the Common Council, and shall be paid out of the highway fund of the proper ward. And the Street Commissioner shall keep and report an accurate and just account of all work so performed, including the sums paid for lumber or other materials, and his own services, charged to the proper ward fund, which accounts shall, when properly certified, be audited by the Controller as now required by law. *Provided,* That the Street Commissioner shall in no case expend upon any street, or in any ward any sum in excess of the amount appropriated as herein provided by the Common Council.

SEC. 6. All Ordinances or parts of Ordinances inconsistent with the provisions of this Ordinance are hereby repealed.

CHAPTER LXIV.

OF THE PAYMENT OF CLAIMS AGAINST THE CITY.

[Ordinance Approved July 18th, 1870.]

SECTION 1. All claims and demands of every name and nature whatever, against the City of East Saginaw, shall in the first instance be presented and filed with the City Controller, who shall inquire into and audit or reject the same and report the same to the Common Council at its next session or as soon thereafter as practicable with a communication in writing, setting forth the facts in relation to the payment thereof.

All claims to be presented and filed with Controller.

His duty.

SEC. 2. All claims or demands against the City, when presented to the Controller, shall be accompanied with an affidavit of the person rendering it, as provided in Section 18, of Title 5, of the City Charter.

Accompan'd with affidavit.

SEC. 3. No person shall deliver goods, property or labor to the City, except upon the order of the Council, and the Controller or other officer legally authorized to purchase or contract for the same as provided in the Charter of said City, any person presenting a claim or demand against the City for supplies furnished for the use of the City or any Officer or Board thereof, shall accompany the same with a bill of the items thereof with the name or names of the person or persons upon and by whose order and for whose use the same were furnished.

No person to deliver goods except upon orders of the Council, etc.

All claims to be accompanied with written statement, etc.

SEC. 4 All claims and demands against the City for work or labor performed for the corporation under any contract for paving any street, lane or alley, or for the construction or repairs of any sewer or drain, side or crosswalk, bridge or culvert, shall be accompanied with a written statement under oath of the amount of work or labor performed and the precise locality or street where such work or labor was performed, and the extent of the same; and before any such claim or demand is presented for allowance to the Controller, it shall be the duty of the City Surveyor or Street Commissioner, or Sewer Board, as the case may be, to ascertain and certify whether said work has been performed agreeable to contract and in the manner and to the extent set forth in the statement accompanying such claim or demand, and has been performed in other respects in a good, substantial and workmanlike manner, and the amount claimed therefor, are reasonable and just, and due claimants under their contract.

No claims to be paid until audited by Controller and allowed by Council.

SEC. 5. No claim or demand against the City of East Saginaw, shall be paid until the same has been audited and allowed by vote of the Common Council of said City, except in cases particularly provided for by Ordinances or the City Charter.

CHAPTER LXV.

OF THE SETTING OUT AND PROTECTING SHADE TREES.

[Ordinance Approved November 22d, 1869.]

Setting out Shade trees.

SECTION 1. Any person owning or occupying any land adjoining any public street in said City, may plant or set out Trees on such street contiguous to his land, which trees shall be set in regular rows at a distance of not less than six feet or more than twenty feet from each other, and on streets ninety-nine feet wide, fifteen feet from the line of lots; on streets sixty feet wide eleven feet from the line of lots. The trees not to be less than eight feet high and not less than one and one half inches in diameter properly set out and protected by stake or guard.

To be credited on Highway tax.

SEC. 2. Any such person owning or occupying land contiguous to any street in said City, as aforesaid, and who is assessed any highway tax, may cause to be paid of such tax a sum not exceeding twenty-five per cent. thereof for any one year by planting or setting out trees during that year under the provisions of this Ordinance, which sum when so paid shall be credited on his highway tax for that year.

SEC. 3. The Street Commissioner shall certify all accounts for setting out or planting trees under the provisions of this Ordinance, which accounts shall be audited by the Controller, such account so audited and certified, presented to any proper officer collecting taxes, shall be his voucher, and such officer shall deduct the amount thereof from such persons highway taxes to be collected by him at that time. *Provided,* That the sum allowed for each tree shall not exceed fifty cents, and that no more than twenty-five per cent of any persons highway tax shall be deducted in any one year. *And provided further*, that such account so certified shall not be transferable, nor shall it be a charge against the City, except as provided for herein. Street Commissioner to certify to and Controller to audit accounts.

SEC. 4. Any person who shall wilfully or maliciously, or without lawful authority cut down, root up, injure, distroy or remove, or in any way deface any living fruit or ornamental tree or trees, or their stacks or guards standing on any street, alley or public grounds of this City, shall upon conviction thereof be fined in any sum not exceeding twenty-five dollars and costs, and in default of the payment of such fine, may be imprisoned in the county jail or City prison not exceeding twenty days. Penalty for wilfully, etc. distroying trees.

SEC. 5. An Ordinance entitled "An Ordinance relative to Shade Trees," made and passed by the Common Council of the City of East Saginaw, July 11th, 1859 is hereby repealed. Repealed.

CHAPTER LXVI.

OF LICENSING TAVERN KEEPERS, &C.

[Ordinance Approved June 5th, 1868.]

No person to keep, etc. tavern without license.

SECTION 1. That no person or firm shall be allowed to open, keep or maintain any Tavern, Inn, Common Victualing House or Saloon, or engage in the business of Tavern Keepers, Inn Holder, Common Victualing or Saloon Keeper within the limits of the City of East Saginaw, without he or they shall have first obtained a license therefor under the provisions of the City Charter and of this Ordinance.

Licenses, how signed, and what to contain.

SEC. 2. That all licenses issued under the provisions of this Ordinance, shall be signed by the Mayor of the City, and countersigned by the City Clerk, and shall have the corporate seal of the City impressed thereon, it shall also set forth the full name of the person or firm obtaining the same, the sum paid therefor the purpose, trade or business for which granted and the number and location of the building or place where such business is to be carried on.

Licenses, when to expire and not transferable

SEC. 3. That all licenses granted under and by virtue of this Ordinance, shall expire on the first day of May, in each year, unless sooner revoked by the Common Council. Such license shall not be transferable to others than the parties originally named therein, nor shall any such license be construed or used to cover any business calling or purpose not expressly set forth and specified therein not to legalize any act or business contrary to or forbidden by any Ordinance of this City or any law of the State.

When more than one license required.

SEC. 4. That in every case where any person or firm shall carry on one or more of the pursuits or occupations specified in this Ordinance or any occupation, pursuit or business for which license is required under any Ordinance of this City at the same time or in the same place a seperate license must be obtained for each purpose, occupation or business.

To give a receipt and amount to pay.

SEC. 5. That every person or firm applying for any license under this Ordinance shall give a receipt for the same, which receipt shall be filed with the City Clerk as a voucher for the delivery of such license for the use of the City of East Saginaw, the following sums of money, to wit: For each Tavern, Inn or Common Victnaling House or Saloon, the sum of ten dollars.

SEC. 6. That all Victualing Houses and Saloons licensed under this act shall be closed at twelve o'clock in the afternoon and not be opened before six o'clock in the forenoon. When Saloons, etc. to be closed and opened.

SEC. 7. That it shall be the duty of the Marshal of the City, as soon as possible after the first day of May in each year, to obtain a list of all persons, firms and houses in said City, who are liable to pay and procure license under this Ordinance, and to require payments of the amounts specified for each and every one of them, and also all others who may become liable for the same at any time during the year, and in case any person shall neglect or refuse to comply with the provisions of this Ordinance. The Marshal shall cause all such persons to be presented for each and every violation of the same as provided in said Section twenty, of Title three, of the act to incorporate the City of East Saginaw, and it shall be the duty of the Chief of Police and of each and every memcer of the Police force of said City, to render all aid required or necessary for the faithful execution of this Ordinance. Duty of the Marshal.

SEC. 8. That all monies received for the use of the City from granting of licenses or fines imposed under this Ordinance, shall be credited to and become a part of the poor fund of said City. When moneys are to be credited.

SEC. 9. That any violation of the provisions of this Ordinance by any person or firm holding license as herein provided, shall be held to forfeit the same, and the power is expressly reserved to the Common Council to revoke any or all licenses granted whenever in the opinion of the majority of said Council, the public good may require such action or be promoted thereby. Common Council can revokelice'se under some circumstances.

SEC. 10. That all Ordinances and parts of Ordinances heretofore passed, which conflict with the provisions of this Ordinance so far as the same may effect or prevent its enforcement are hereby repealed. Repealed.

CHAPTER LXVII.

OF THE ASSESSMENT AND COLLECTION OF TAXES.

[Ordinance Approved October 3d, 1859.]

Controller to levy taxes.

SECTION 1. When the assessment roll shall be delivered by the Supervisors to the Controller; the said Controller shall levy the tax as certified to him by the City Clerk, and such other sums as may be required by law.

Marshal's fees for collecting taxes

SEC. 2. For collecting the taxes on the tax roll of the City, the Marshal shall be entitled to per centage at the rate of four per cent. upon the whole sum to be collected by him and the Controller shall add that sum in the computation of taxes in each year.

As amended by an Ordinance passed April 15th, 1861.

SEC. 3. In extending the taxes upon the assessment roll, the Controller shall have one column for City taxes for general purposes, which shall include the sinking fund and library tax; and one column for the City highway tax, and one column for the School tax, in which shall be placed all School taxes, and in case there are any special assessments to be collected, the same shall be placed in a separate column, and the Controller shall note in the margin what such special assessment is for, and the date when the same was levied, and the same shall be levied only on the property originally assessed. *Provided*, That the said Ordinance as hereby amended shall apply only to the manner of levying, extending and collecting the City taxes as herein mentioned.

Re-assessed taxes to be made in red ink. And all re-assessments shall be made in the same description of property first assessed

SEC. 4. All taxes reassessed shall be entered with red ink in the column of taxes to which it belongs above the tax for the year in which said reassessment shall be made is used, and said entry shall also show in red ink the year for which such tax is reassessed. All reassessments shall be in the same description of property first assessed and shall not extend to any other.

CHAPTER LXVIII.

OF REGULATING AND RESTRAINING HAWKING AND PEDDLING.

[Ordinance Approved July 10th, 1871.]

SECTION 1. That Section one of an Ordinance entitled an Ordinance to restrain Hawking and Peddling, made and passed by the Common Council of the City of East Saginaw, June 11th, 1866, be amended so as to read as follows:

SECTION 1. Each and every transient, or other person or persons, having in his, her or their possession any goods, wares or merchandise, brought to or purchased in said City, to be disposed of by Hawking or Peddling in the streets thereof, shall, before selling, or exposing for sale any such goods, wares or merchandise as aforesaid, apply to the City Clerk for a license therefor, and shall before receiving such license pay to said Clerk for the use of said City, the following sums: Each and every transient person the sum of five dollars for the first five days and two dollars for each day thereafter; and each and every resident of said City who shall have been a resident thereof for five months next preceding the time of making such application, and who shall be of the age of fifty years or upwards, the sum of six dollars per annum, and each and every other resident thereof for the period of six months next preceding the time of making such application the sum of three dollars per week.

AN ORDINANCE,

Relative to the appointment of

COMMISSIONERS OF WATER WORKS,

And the Duties of such Commissioners.

Be it Ordained, by the Common Council of the City of East Saginaw, as follows:

SECTION 1. The Common Council shall appoint within twenty days after the adoption of this Ordinance, six suitable persons, Water Commissioners, who shall constitute and be known as the Board of Water Commissioners of the City of East Saginaw. Said Commissioners shall continue in office for the following terms: The term of office of two of said Commissioners shall expire on the first Monday of May, A. D., 1873: the term of other two of said Commissioners on the first Monday of May, A. D., 1874; and the term of the other two of said Commissioners on the first Monday of May, A. D., 1875, and the term for which each one is appointed shall be designated in the resolution of appointment; and in the month of May in each year thereafter there shall be appointed two Water Commissioners who shall hold their office for term of three years, and who shall qualify as is hereinafter provided. Said Commissioners shall be freeholders in and residents of this city, but no two of said Commissioners shall be residents of the same Ward. Each Commissioner shall continue in office until his successor is appointed and shall qualify. In case of vacancy in office by death, removal, resignation or other inability to serve, the Common Council shall immediately fill the vacancy for the unexpired term.

SEC. II. Every Commissioner shall, before entering upon the duties of his office, and within ten days after notice of appointment, take and file with the City Clerk, the constitutional oath of this State, and shall also enter into a bond to the city with sureties to be approved by the Common Council, conditioned for the faithful performance of his duties as such Commissioner, the penalty of the bond each Commissioner shall be the sum of one thousand dollars

SEC. III. A meeting of the majority of the Board of Commissioners shall be necessary for the transaction of business, though a meeting of less than a majority shall have authority to constitute a legal adjournment.

SEC. IV. The said Water Commissioners shall, as soon after their appointment in each year as may be, organize as a Board by the election of one of their own number as President, and shall appoint a Water Works Engineer, and other necessary employees. The City Clerk shall act as Secretary of the Board, and keep the records, plans and papers of the Board. The records, plans and papers of the Board shall at all times be open to the inspection o any member of the Common Council, or any tax payer of the city. The salary and pay of the Water Works Engineer and the other necessary employees shall be such as the Board of Water Commissioners shall by resolution direct, and the Common Council approve.

SEC. V The said Board of Water Commissioners shall, as soon after their appointment as may be, devise and frame a plan of supplying the city with pure and wholesome water; and they shall submit to the Common Council such plans as in their opinion may be most feasible for obtaining such supply of water, and said plans shall embrace proper distribution pipes and supplies for all streets and places where in their opinion it shall be of interest to the city. Upon such plan being confirmed and adopted by the Common Council, it shall be certified to by the City Clerk, and filed in the office of the Board of Water Commissioners, whereupon the plan, therein set forth, shall become the permanent plan of supplying the city with water, subject to be changed only by the recommendation of said Board and the approval of a majority of the Common Council elect certified and filed as herein provided.

SEC. VI. The said Board shall, upon the filing of said plans, recommend to the Common Council the construction of such hydraulic works, the purchase of such real estate upon which to erect such works, the laying and construction of such distribution pipes and the doing of such other work connected therewith, as said Board shall deem necessary to be done in that year, and shall in the month of April in each year hereafter report to the Common Council what distribution pipes should be constructed, and what other work connected with said Water Works they deem necessary to be performed in that year; and they shall accompany said report with an estimate in detail of the probable cost of whatever is therein recommended. The Common Council shall thereupon consider said report, and they may reject the same or adopt it in whole or in part, and their action therein shall be certified to the Board of Water Commissioners by the City Clerk.

SEC. VII. Upon the adoption of said report of the Water Commissioners in whole or in part, the Common Council shall order so much of said work as has been approved to be done, and shall proceed to advertise for proposals to do the work so ordered under such specifications and forms as the Board of Water Commissioners shall deem necessary, which advertisement shall be published at least fifteen days in the paper contracted with to do the city printing, and shall state the time and place when and where such proposals shall be received, and the work so advertised shall if awarded be given to the lowest bidder, who will give good and sufficient security for the furnishing sufficient and suitable material therefor, and the prompt and faithful execution of such work. The Common Council shall have the right to reject any and all bids. But the said Board of Water Commissioners shall in no case proceed with the construction of any work of the amount of one hundred dollars and upwards, except upon advertisements for proposals for the construction of the same, as hereinafter provided. *Provided,* nevertheless, that the Common Council may, by a vote of two-thirds of all the members elect, authorize said Board to enter into such contracts without advertising.

SEC. VIII No Commissioner shall be directly or indirectly interested in any contract relating to the work or the materials therefor, nor in any work or materials for the work, nor for any portion of the Water Works; nor shall any Commissioner be surety on the bond of any person contracting to do any work or furnish any materials connected in any way with said Water Works.

SEC. IX. All work contracted to be done as aforesaid shall be under the control and supervision of the said Board of Water Commissioners, and the said Commissioners and all others acting under their authority shall have the right to use the ground or soil under any street, alley or publi space for the purpose of introducing water into and through any and all portions of the city on condition that they shall cause the surface of such streets, alleys or public spaces to be relaid and restored to its usual state, and all damages done thereto to be repaired.

SEC. X. The connecting or supply pipes leading from buildings or yards to the distribution pipes, shall be inserted from the curb line of the street, and kept in repair at the expense of the owner or occupant of the building or yard, and shall not be inserted or connected with the main pipe, until a permit therefor shall be obtained from said Commissioners o other person having charge thereof; and all such connecting or supply pipes shall be constructed in the manner directed by said Commissioners to the person in charge.

SEC. XI. Said Board shall certify to the amount due upon all contracts and for all materials furnished and labor performed in constructing or repairing said Water Works, and all bills and accounts thus certified for amounts so due shall be audited by the Comptroller, and presented by him to the Common Council in the same manner as other bills and accounts against said city.

The City Treasurer shall be Treasurer of said Board of Water Commissions, and it shall be his duty to open in his books a Water Works account, which account shall exhibit all amounts paid into said fund, either loans, water rents or taxes, and also all amounts expended on account of said fund.

SEC. XII. The said Commissioners shall have power from time to time to make and establish such By-Laws, Rules and Regulations as they shall judge proper as to the duties of their officers and employees, and as to the means of enforcing said duties, and for the regulation of the time and manner of holding meetings of the Commissioners, and for the enforcing of the water rents and the manner of using water, and generally for transacting, managing and directing the affairs of the Commissioners; and they may provide regulations as to water used, water and water rents, and enforce the observance thereof by cutting off the use and supply of water. *Provided*, That such By-Laws, Rules and Regulations are first submitted to the Common Council and are approved and adopted by that body.

SEC XIII. The said Commissioners shall establish a scale of rents to be charged and paid to the Commissioners from time to time, either in advance or at such time and times as the Commissioners shall prescribe for the supply of water, to be called water rents, and apportioned to the different classes of buildings in the city in reference to their ordinary or extraordinary uses for dwellings, stores, shops, hotels, factories, livery stables, barns and all other buildings, establishments and trades, yards, number of families or occupants or consumption of water, as near as may be practicable, which scale of water rents shall be submitted to the Common Council for their approval and adoption; and said Commissioners and their respective employees shall be authorized at all times to enter into any building or place where water is used from supply pipes, to examine as to the water, quantity of water used, and manner of using it.

SEC. XIV. The said Commissioners shall annually on the first Monday of March in each year, and at all such times as required by the Common Council, deliver to the Common Council a detailed statement of all their work and condition of their affairs and state of finances, including a full detail of the amount expended in the progress of the work, and a particular statement of any deficiency as to the water rents, as to meeting the interest upon so much of the bonded indebtedness of the city as was created for the purpose of erecting water works.

Made and passed by the Common Council of the City of East Saginaw, Michigan, this 29th day of January A. D. 1872.

L. SIMONEAU, Mayor.

Attest: ASAHEL CHASE, City Clerk.

INDEX

TO THE

ORDINANCES

OF THE

CITY OF EAST SAGINAW

INDEX.

PAGE.

ACCIDENTS.

Ordinance relative to prevention of - 48

ALDERMEN.

May direct Physician to attend sick, - - - 13

Marshal to serve papers delivered to him by 8

Sidewalks not to be obstructed notified to remove by 40

Person having charge of team, horse, &c., to obey orders of 46

Powers relative to privies, &c., - - - - 79

Ex-officio Fire Wardens, - - - - - 85

Certain members of Board of Health, - - 61

Permission in writing to Prison Keeper, - - 82

ALLEYS, see Streets.

ANIMALS, see "Streets, Lamps, Dead Animals, Pounds, Sidewalks."

ASHES

Depositing in Streets prohibited, - - - 69

Secured in proper vessels, - - - 93

ASSESSMENT ROLLS.

Where kept when not in use, - - - 18

By whom made, - - - - . - 18

To whom delivered when completed, - - 19

For construction of sidewalks, - - - 36

Street Commissioner to make in certain cases, - 15

ASSESSOR.

Appointment of - - - - - - - 18

Oath and bond of - - - - - - 18

Term of office, - - - - - - - 18

General powers and duties, - - - - 18–19

May require assistance of Surveyor, - - - 18

To prepare Tax Roll, - - - - - 19

To preserve books, &c., - - - - - 19

Sewer Commissioners shall give notice to of Sewer connections; - - - - - - - 122

ASSISTANT ENGINEER, see "Fire Department."

How appointed, - - - - - - 85

General powers and duties, - - 85-86-87-88-89-90

PAGE

ATTORNEY.
General powers and duties, - - - - - 5
Opinions to be in writing, - - - - - 5
To appear as Attorney in behalf of City, - - 5
In opening Streets, - - - - - - 6
In behalf of officers of City, - - - - - 6
Will act as member of Committee, - - 6
To Certify to Bonds, Deeds, &c., - - - 6
Prepare draft of Ordinance, - - - 6
To make report of suits, - - - - - 6
Appointment and term of office, - - - 7
To keep Register and deliver papers to successor, - 7
Shall act as legal adviser to Board of Health when requested, - - - - - - - 61
Permission in writing by, to the Jail Keeper, - 82
Duty to draw Sewer Contracts, - - - 121

AUCTIONS.
Of impounding animals, - - - 104

AUCTIONEERS.
Ordinance relative to - - - - - 55–56

AWNINGS, see Streets.

BAIL.
For appearance in Recorder's Court, - - 80–82

BALL ALLEYS.
Keeping open on Sunday prohibited, - - 115
Ordinance relative to - - - - - - 115

BALCONIES, see Streets.

BALUSTRADES, see Streets.

BARRIERS.
Shall be erected to provide against accidents, - 48
Contractors liable for penalty for not erecting - 49

BATHING.
Prohibited in river, - - - - 76

BEER HALLS.
Gaming in prohibited - - - - 116

BELL RINGING.
In Streets prohibited, - - - - - 57

BILLIARD ROOMS.
Keeping open on Sunday prohibited, - - 115
Keepers of, to be licensed, - - - 114
Gaming in, prohibited, - - - 115

BILLIARDS.
Gambling with, prohibited, - - - 115

PAGE

BOARD OF HEALTH.
Ordinance relative to - - - - - - 61
Who to compose Board, - - - - 61
City Clerk, Clerk of Board, - - - - - 61
City Attorney to act as legal adviser, - - 61
Powers relative to Privies, Vaults, &c., - - 62
Marshal and his Assistants shall attend sessions, 8

BOARD OF SEWER COMMISSIONERS.
Time of Appointment and Term of Office, - - 119
Power to Elect President, - - - 119
Sewer Engineer to act as Secretary, - - - 119
General pawers and duties, - - - 119–122

BOATS AND CARS.
Ordinance relative to Porters and Runners, - 113

BONDS.
Attorney to certify to form of - - - - 6
Of Attorney, - - - - - - 7
Of Marshal, - - - - - - - 10
Of Street Commissioner, - - - - - 16
Of City Surveyor, - - - - - - 14
Of City Clerk, - - - - - - 13
Of Policemen, - - - - - - - 10
Of Assessor, - - - - - - 18
Of Ward Collectors, - - - - - - 19
Of Director of Poor, - - - - - 21
Of City Scavenger, - - - - - - 25
Of Inspector of Gas Meters, - - - - 26
Of Harbor Master, - - - - - - 51
Of Pawn Broker, - - - - - - 58
Of Pound Master, - - - - - - 103

BUILDINGS, see Streets.
Wooden prohibited within fire limits, - - 91
Plan of erecting buildings within fire limits, - 91
Size of building limited, - - - - - - 91
Consent of Council to repair, - - - 92
To prohibit repairing buildings when more than half of its value is distroyed, - - - - - 92
Shall have Scuttles, - - - - - 94
Fire Marshals may enter and examine, - - 94
Renting of, for Gaming prohibited, - - 116
Buildings not to be moved in streets without permission, 41

BUILDING MATERIAL, see Sireets.

BUTCHER SHOPS, see Slaughter Houses.

PAGE.

CATTLE.
Not to be herded in streets, - - - - - 43
Cattle Troughs not to be placed in streets. - 43
Provisions relative to impounding, - - 103–106

CELLAR DOORS, see Streets.

CEMETERIES.
Ordinance relative to - - - - - 66

CHIEF ENGINEER.
Appointment of - - - - - - 85
General powers and duties, - - 85–90–96

CHIMNEYS.
Shall be cleaned out, - - - - - 93
Constructing of - - - - - 93

CHURCHES.
Disturbing worship in, prohibited, - - - 73

CLAIMS.
Payment of against the City, - - - 139

CITY CLERK.
Shall post card with name of Physician, - 11
Appointment, how made. - - - - - 12
His duties, - - - - - - - - 12
Fees in certain case, - - - - - - 13
Bond, - - - - - - - - 13
To notify persons to be assessed building sidewalks, 36
Hawkers and Peddlers to obtain license from, - 55
Transient Auctioneers to obtain license from, - 56
Clerk of the Board of Health, - - - - 61
Notify persons of assessment to fill up low lots. - 65
To license Drays, - - - - - - - 110

CLERK OF THE RECORDER'S COURT, see Recorder's Court.

CONTRACTS
Attorney to draw and certify, - - - - 6
Controller shall make in certain cases, - - 16

CONSTABLES.
General powers and duties of - - 7–10–28–31
Under direction of the Marshal. - - - - 8
Cause for removal, - - - - - 9–31
Bonds of - - - - - - - - 10
To attend fires. - - - - - - - 10
Shall serve papers relating to business of City, delivered by Mayor, &c., - - - - - - - 8
Shall serve process of Recorder's Court, - - 80
Shall return process to Clerk of Recorder's Court, 81
Penalty for resisting, - - - - - - 81
Duties of at fires, - - - - - - - 89
Shall enforce Ordinances relative to prevention of fires. 95

PAGE.

CONTROLLER.
Shall countersign Bonds, - - - - 16
Examine all claims against City, - - - 16
Purchase all supplies and materials, - - 16
Shall examine the Tax Rolls and Returns of City Officers, 17
Shall keep complete set of books, - - - 17
Shall open account with the different Officers, - 17
Power to extend Special Assessment Roll, - - 17
Power of Assistant Controllers, - - - 17
To procure for Assessor all books, &c., - - 19
Tax Roll to be delivered to Controller, - - 19–144
Ward Collector to file Statement with - - 19
Director of the Poor shall report to, as to Supplies, 21
Shall advertise for proposals for Supplies for Poor, 22
Shall procure Railroad tickets for paupers, - 23
Countersign Cemetery Deeds, - - - 67
Application to be made to Controller to purchase lot in Cemetery, - - - - - - - 66
To keep a Register of all lots sold, - - 67
To examine complaints and report to Mayor any violation of Ordinance relative to Fire Engines, &c., - - 98
Shall make Pay Roll for paid hand Engine Company, 100
Shall make Pay Roll for paid Hook & Ladder Company, 102
Pound Master shall report to - - : 105
Proposals for building Sewers, to be opened in Controller's office, - - - - - - - - 121
Shall audit Sewer accounts, - - - - 121
Shall examine and audit all claims, - - 139
No goods to be delivered except upon order of - 139
Shall audit accounts under Ordinance for setting out and protecting Shade Trees, - - - - 141

COSTS.
Clerk of Recorder's Court may demand security for, 79
When complainant to pay, - - - 80
Execution for - - - - - - 80
Fees in Recorder's Court, - - - 83

CROSSWALKS, see Sidewalks.
How constructed, - - - - 39
Provide funds for constructing, - - - 36
Leaving Horses, &c. on crosswalks prohibited, - 41

CROWDS, see Streets.
In front of Churches prohibited, - - - 74

DEAD ANIMALS.
Regulations relative to - - - - 69
Fees of Scavenger for removing, - - - 26

PAGE

DIRECTOR OF THE POOR.
General powers and duties, - - - - - 21
Office hours, - - - - - - 21
Bond, - - - - - - - - 21
May direct Physician to attend sick, - - 11
DIVINE WORSHIP.
Disturbance of prohibited - - - - - 73
DISORDERLY CONDUCT.
Ordinance relative to - - - - - 74
Prohibited in Engine House, - - - - - 98
DOCKS.
Ordinance relative to - - - - - 53
DOGS.
Ordinance relative to - - - - - 106
Tax on Dogs, - - - - - - 106
Dogs to be muzzled, - - - - - - 108
Dogs to be impounded, - - - - - 107
DRAINS, see Sewers.
DRAYS.
Ordinance relative to - - - - - 110
Stands for - - - - - - - - 109
DRUNKEN AND DISORDERLY PERSONS.
How punished, - - - - - - 75
May be required to give security for good behavior, 75
Executions from Recorder's Court, - - 80
FAST DRIVING, see Streets.
FISH.
Putrid deposited in streets prohibited, - - 70
FIRE DEPARTMENT.
Ordinance relative to - - - - - 85
Who shall constitute, - - - - - 85
Appointment of Chief and Assistant Engineers, - 85
Duties of Engineers, - - - - - 86
Power of Chief Engineer, - - - - - 86
Duties of Chief Engineer, - - - - 86
Division of Fire Engine Men, - - - - 87
Duties of Hook and Ladder and Axe men, - 87
Certificate to appointment of member to be countersigned by the Clerk, - - - - - - 88
Badge of office of the members of Common Council, 88
Chief Engineer to wear badge, - - - - 88
Assistant Engineer to wear badge, - - - - 88
How Fire Wardens to be distinguished, - - 89
Cap of Foreman and Assistants, how marked, - 89
Penalty for disobedience of orders at fire, - 89

PAGE.

FIRE DEPARTMENT,—(*Continued.*)
Penalty for refusing to help draw Engine, &c., - 89
Marshal and Constables to repair to fires, - 89
Hook, Ladder and Axe Men to be under the direction of Chief Engineer, - - - - - - 90
All fines for disobedience to Ordinance to enure to benefit of Fire Department, - - - - - 90
Engine not to be used for private purposes without consent of Mayor, &c., - - - - - - 90
Care of property at fires, - - - - - 90
Of Steam Fire Engine Companies, - - 96
Of Paid Hand Engine Companies, - - - 99
Of Hook and Ladder Companies, - - 101
Spirituous liquors not allowed in Engine House, - 98
Tippling, rioting or immoral conduct in, prohibited, 98-100-102

FIRE LIMITS.
Designation of - - - - - 91-96
Common Council may extend by resolution, - 92

FIRE WARDENS.
Shall be members of the Fire Department, - - 85
Members of the Common Council are ex-officio Fire Wardens, - - - - - - - 85
How appointed, - - - - - - 85
Duties of Fire Wardens, - - - - 85
Badge of office, - - - - - - 89

FIRES.
Ordinance relative to the prevention and extinguishment of 91
Method and place of erecting buildings within fire limits, 91
Size of wooden buildings limited, - - - 91
Consent of Common Council to repair buildings partially destroyed, - - - - - - 92
To prohibit the repairing of buildings in certain cases, 92
Permission to build or repair in certain cases, - 92
Every wrecked building allowed to remain contrary to Ordinance a distinct offence, - - - 93
Prohibiting the manufacture of turpentine, &c., 93
Hay and Straw to be secured, - - - 93
To secure shavings, - - - - - 93
To secure lights, - - - - - 93
Construction of Chimneys, - - - 93
Method of putting up stove pipe, - - - 93
Chimneys and stove pipes to be cleaned, - 93
Not to carry fire unsecured, - - - - - 93
Not to deposit ashes unless secured in proper vessels or ash house, - - - - - - 94

PAGE.

FIRES,—(*Continued.*)

Not to kindle fires in Streets, &c., - - 94
Regulate the use of fire arms, - - - 94
Provisions for scuttle and stairway, - - 94
To regulate the storing of gunpowder, - - 94
How gunpowder to be carried through the streets, 94
Duty of Marshal, - - - - - - 94
Regulations as to Propellers, &c., - - 95
Who liable when offence committed by servants, - 95
Duty of Marshal and Constables to make complaint, 95

FIREWOOD, see Inspector of Firewood.

GAMES.

Playing of in streets, prohibited, - - - 44
Gambling prohibited, - - - - - 115

GAS LIGHTS, see Inspectors of Gas Meters, Lamps and Ordinance establishing Gas Works to the City of East Saginaw.

GAS METERS, see Inspector of Gas Meters.

GOODS, see Streets and Harbor Masters.

GUNPOWDER.

Regulations relative to storing, - - - - 94
Carrying in streets unless secured, prohibited, - 94

HAND BILLS.

Posting without permission prohibited, - - 137

HAND ENGINE COMPANIES.

Paid, Ordinance relative to, - - - - - 99

HARBOR MASTER.

Appointment of - - - - - - 51
Bond of - - - - - - - 51
Salary of - - - - - - - 51
General powers and duties, - - - - 51

HAWKERS AND PEDDLERS.

Ordinance relative to - - - - - 145
Transient Auctioneers, - - - - - 56

HEALTH, see Board of Health.

HIDES.

Not to remain in streets, - - - - - 70

HOOK AND LADDER COMPANIES.

Paid, Ordinance relative to - - - - 101
Under direction of Chief Engineer, - - 101

HORSES.

Herding of in streets prohibited, - - - - 43
Troughs for feeding or watering in streets prohibited, 43
Impounding of - - - - - - 103

ILL FAME.

Ordinance relative to - - - - 77

PAGE.

INDECENT.
- Language or conduct prohibited, - - 73
- Exposure prohibited, - - - - - 74
- Books and Pictures prohibited, - - - - 74

INSPECTORS OF FIREWOOD.
- Appointment and term of office, - - - - 24
- Fees of - - - - - - - - 24
- Powers and duties, - - - - - 24

INSPECTOR OF GAS METERS.
- Appointment and term of office, - - - - 26
- Salary of and how paid, - - - - - 27
- Bond of - - - - - - - 27
- Office of - - - - - - - 27
- General powers and duties, - - - - 27
- Shall have charge of Lamps, &c., - - 27
- To keep books, - - - - - 28
- How suspended, - - - - - 28

JURORS.
- Fees of in Recorder's Court, - - - - 83
- For opening streets, - - - - - 83

LAMPS, see Inspector of Gas Meters, Streets.
- Lighting or extinguishing prohibited, - - 47
- Putting up without permission prohibited, - 47
- Hitching Animals to posts of prohibited, - - 47
- Injuries to prohibited, - - - - - 47
- Under control of Mayor, - - - - - 47
- Duty of Marshal and Policemen, - - - - 48

LICENSES.
- General Ordinance relative to - - 116
- To Hawkers and Peddlers, - - - 145–55
- To Transient Auctioneers, - - - - 56
- To Pawnbrokers, - - - - - - 58
- To Draymen, - - - - - - 110
- To Porters and Runners, - - - - 112
- To Ball Alleys, - - - - - - 114
- To Billiard Tables, - - - - - - 114
- To Shows, - - - - - - - 116
- To Tavern Keepers, - - - - - - 142
- To Saloon Keepers, - - - - - 142
- To Victualing Houses, - - - - - 142

LIVERY STABLES.
- Nuisance in and about prohibited, - - - 70

LOTTERIES.
- Prohibited, - - - - - - 115

PAGE.

MARSHAL.

Bond of - - - - - - - - 10
Office and office hours, - - - - - 8
General powers and duties, - - - 7-10-28
To serve process, - - - - - - - 7
To obey and execute precepts, - - - 7
To attend sessions of Recorder's Court, - 8
To be Chief of Police, - - - - 8
To attend fires, - - - - - - - 10-89
Duty under Street Ordinance. - - - 47
Power to direct cleaning of privies, - - 25
Fees of Marshal in certain cases, - - - 32
How claims for fees to be presented, - - 33
Duties of Marshal relative to Lamps and Lamp Posts, 48
To have control of Lamp Posts, - - - - 47
To be one of Board of Health, - - - - 61
Marshal return of process in Recorder's Court, - 81
Fees of Marshal in Recorder's Court, - - 83
Duty under Ordinance relative to the Prevention of Fires, 94-95
To construct Pounds when directed, - - 103
Duty under Ordinance relative to Dogs, - 106
Duty to destroy Gaming instruments, - - 116
Duty for violation of Ordinance relative to Shows, 118
Duty under Ordinance for filling low grounds, - 126
Duty of Marshal to enforce Ordinance relative to punishment of offences by hard labor, - - - - 136
Duty under Ordinance relative to Licenses, Tavern Keepers, &c., - - - - - - - - - 142
May inspect books of Pawnbrokers, - - - 58
Duty of Pawnbroker to notify in certain cases, - 59
Penalty for resisting in serving process, - 29

MAYOR.

May direct Physician to attend sick, - - - 11
Shall investigate complaints against Physician, - 12
Mayor's duties under Ordinance of Director of Poor. 21
Duty under Ordinance of Chief Scavenger, - - 25
May suspend Inspector of Gas Meters, - - 28
Police, &c., to act under direction of - - - 28
Chief of Police to assign beats for Policemen under direction of Mayor, - - - - - - 29
With Chief of Police to assign hours of duty, 30
May suspend Policeman, - - - - - 31
Shall sign warrants for collection of Sidewalk Assessments, 37
Powers to remove goods, &c., from Sidewalks when notified by - - - - - - - - • 40

PAGE

MAYOR,—(*Continued.*)

No person to remove building across street without permission of - - - - - - - 43

Building material not to be deposited on Sidewalk without permission, - - - - - - 41

Building material not to be deposited in Streets without permission, - - - - - - - 42

Pavement, &c., not to be dug up, &c., without permission of - - - - - - - - - 42

Buildings not to be removed through Streets without permission, - - - - - - - 46

To have control of Lamps and Lamp Posts, - 47

Bell Ringing in streets prohibited without permission of 57

Pawn Brokers books to be open to the inspection of 59

Mayor to execute deed to Lots in Cemeteries, - 67

Duty to prevent nuisances, - - - 71

Recommendation of members for Paid Fire Engine Companies, - - - - - - - - 49

Recommendation of members for Paid Hook and Ladder Company, - - - - - - 105

Complaints to be made to - - - - 100

Power to license Porters and Runners, - - 112

Power to license Shows, &c., - - - - 116

Persons arrested may be discharged by, - - 118

Licenses of Tavern Keepers to be signed by - 142

NUISANCES.

Abatement of by filling low grounds, - 126

Duties of Board of Health in respect to - 62

Ordinance relative to - - - - 69

ORDINANCES.

To be drawn by Attorney, - - - - - 6

To provide for the establishing of Gas Works in the City, 132

Relative to the payment of claims against the City, 139

Relative to the division and expending af the Highway Fund, - - - - - - - - - 137

Providing for the punishment of certain crimes and offences at hard labor, - - - - - 136

Relative to enforcing the Ordinances of the City, 135

Relative to the sale of liquor on election day, - 77

Relative to public decency, - - - 76

Relative to Disorderly Persons, - - 74

Relative to public peace, - - - - 73

PAWNBROKERS.

Ordinance relative to - - - 58

PAGE.

PHYSICIAN.
Appointment of - - - - - - 11
Powers and duties, - - - - - - 11
Is a member of the Board of Health, - - 61
To vaccinate without charge, - - - 11
Complaints against, - - - - 12
Substitute in case of absence, - - - 12
PLACARDS.
Posting of offensive prohibited, - - - 70
Posting on public or private buildings prohibited, 137
POLICE.
Marshal to act as Chief of - - - - 8
POLICEMEN.
Bond of - - - - - - - - 11
Harbor Master to have powers of - - - 52
Pound Master to have power of - - - 106
Duty to destroy Gaming Instruments, - - 116
Uniforming Policemen and their duties in certain cases, 29
Time of duty, - - - - - - 29
Penalty for resisting, - - - - - 29
POUNDS.
Ordinance relative to - - - - - 103
For Dogs, - - - - - - - 106
POUND MASTERS.
Appointment, - - - - - - 103
Term of office, - - - - - - - 103
Bond and oath of office, - - - - 103
Fees of - - - - - - - - 105
General powers and duties, - - - 103-106
PORTERS AND RUNNERS.
Ordinance relative to - - - - - - 112
PRIVIES, see Scavengers.
Regulations respecting, - - - - 71-72-26
PROSTITUTES.
Houses for the resort of prohibited, - - - 77
PUBLIC PEACE.
Ordinance relative to - - - - - 73-74-75-76
RAILING.
Provisions requiring, - - - - - - 45
RECORDER'S COURT.
Marshal and Assistants shall serve process from - 80
Marshal shall attend sessions, - - - - 8
Ordinance relative to - - - - - - 79
Ordinance relative to fees in - - - - 83
Powers relative to persons convicted in - - 82

PAGE.

RIOTS.
Prohibited, - - - - - - - 73

RUNNERS, see Porters and Runners.

SAGINAW RIVER.
Ordinance relative to Harbor Masters, - - 50
Depositing substance in prohibited, - - 50
No Vessel to be moored to bridge, - - - 50
Raft of logs fastened to docks without consent prohibited. 51
Unloading Water Crafts on Sunday prohibited, - 52
Nuisances committed in prohibited, - - 17

SALOONS.
Keep'ng open on Sunday, prohibited, - - 76
Gambling in prohibited, - - - - - 115
Licensing, - - - - - - - - 142

SCAVENGERS.
Ordinance relative to - - - - 25

SEWERS, see Board of Sewer Commissioners.
General provisions relative to, - - - 122
Surveyors shall make surveys for and superintend construction of - - - - - - 13–122
Connections with, - - - - - 42–122
Tax for draining into, - - - - 123

SEXTON CITY.
Appointment of and term of office, - - - 66
Fees of - - - - - - - 66
Duties of - - - - - - - 66–67
May be removed by Cemetery Commissioners, - 68

SHOWS.
On Sundays prohibited, - - - - 76–117
Exhibitions of without license, prohibited, - - 117

SIDEWALKS.
Council shall direct of what material built, - 35
Owners authorized to plank under direction of Marshal, 35
Assessments, how made, - - - - 36
Assessments to be made, - - - - 36
Condition of Assessment Roll, - - - 36
City Clerk to notify persons to be assessed. - - 36
What additional notice required, - - 37
How assessments collected, - - - - - 37
Common Council to hear objections to said assessment roll, 38
Resolution to be offered in, - - - - - 38
Of what material to be constructed, - - 38
Duty of Street Commissioner when Council directs the construction of - - - - - - 39
Widths of Sidewalks, - - - - - 39
When Marshal to construct, - - - - 39

PAGE.

SIDEWALKS,—(*Continued.*)

Mistakes in designating property, - - 39
Cross Walks, how constructed, - - - 39
How Sidewalks to be repaired, - - - 40
Leading or driving animals on, prohibited, - - 40–41
Not to be obstructed, - - - - - 40
Leaving Goods, Wares or Merchandise on - - 40
Sale of Goods upon, prohibited, - - - 43
Sliding or Skating upon, prohibited, - - 46

SIGNS, see Streets.

SLAUGHTERING HOUSES.

Regulations respecting, - - - - - 70

SNOW AND ICE.

Occupants shall remove, - - - - 41

SOAP FACTORIES.

Regulations respecting, - - - - 69

STABLES.

Nuisances in, prohibited, - - - - 70
Lights in, to be secured in lanterns, - - - 93

STANDS, see Sidewalks aud Drays.

STEAMBOATS, see Harbor Masters.

Regulations relative to, - - - - 95

STEAM FIRE ENGINE COMPANIES.

Ordinance relative to - - - - - 96

STORES AND SHOPS.

Keeping open on Sundays prohibited, - - 76
Gambling in, prohibited, - - - 115

STRAW.

Depositing in Streets prohibited, - - 43
Shall be protected from sparks, - - - - 43

STREETS.

Snow and Ice to be removed from Sidewalks, - 41
Buildings not to be removed in, without permission, 41
Animals not to be driven on Sidewalks, - - 41
Building material not to remain on Sidewalks, 41
Streets and Wharfs not to be obstructed, - - 41
Vehicles not to stand in, - - - - - 42
Building material not to be placed in, without permission, 42
Animals to be tied, - - - - - 42
Digging up pavement, prohibited, - - - - 42
Drains and Gutters to be kept clean, - - 43
Straw, &c., not to be thrown in - - - - 43
Stone Masons not to obstruct, - - - 43
Cattle not to be herded in, - - - - - 43

PAGE.

STREETS,—(*Continued.*)

Exhibitions of Stud Horses prohibited, - - 43
Fast driving prohibited, - - - - - 43
Balustrades and Balconies, how constructed, - 44
Games not to be played in - - - - - 44
Gathering in crowds prohibited, - - - - 44
No buildings removed on, without consent, - 46
No buildings to be removed on planked or paved streets. 46
Omnibus not to pass one another in certain cases, 46
Teams not to be left unhitched, - - - 46
Funeral procession not to be interrupted, - - 46
Certain streets not to be occupied for the sale of wood, 46
Duty of Marshal to enforce Ordinance, - - 47
Regulations as to porches, cellar doors and drains, 45
Hoisting goods from, prohibited, - - - 45
Earthen pots not to be placed in windows, - 45
Provisions as to awnings and posts in - - 45
Bathing in sight of spectators, prohibited, - 45
Fire carried in, to be secured, - - - 93
Kindling of Fires in, prohibited, - - - 94
Explosions of fireworks, &c. in, prohibited, - 94
Stands for Drays, - - - - - 109
Gambling in, prohibited, - - - - 115
Lamps suspended without permission over streets, &c., prohibited, - - - - - - - 47

STREET COMMISSIONER.

Duties of under Ordinance, - - - - 15
To file statement with Controller, - - 15
To make Monthly reports, - - - - 15
To make Assessment, - - - - 15
To make report to Common Council, - - 15
Bond and oath of office, - - - - 16
Duties more fully defined, - - - - 16
Duties in the construction of Sidewalks, - 35
Duties in construction of Crosswalks, - - 39
Duties in the repairing of Sidewalks, - - 40
Duty to serve notice of construction of Sidewalks, 37

STREET RAILWAYS.

Ordinance granting permission to establish, - 128

STUD HORSES, see Streets.

SUNDAY.

Ordinance relative to observance of - - 76

PAGE.

SURVEYOR.

General powers and duties, - - - - - 13

Duty under Ordinance relative to private drains and sewers, 122

To superintend the construction and alteration of drains and make report, - - - - - - - 13

To make all plans and specifications for streets, 13

To make survey and give information to officers of City, &c., 14

To keep places, &c. in his office, - - - - 14

Salary, - - - - - - - - 14

Bond, - - - - - - - 14

Assessor may require the services of, in certain cases, 18

Shall designate grade of drain, - - - - 126

SWIMMING, see Bathing.

TALLOW CHANDLERS.

Regulations respecting, - - - - - 69

TAVERNS.

Gaming in, prohibited, - - - - - 115

To be licensed, - - - - - - 142

TREES.

Setting out Shade Trees, - - - - - 140

Credit on Tax, - - - - - - 140

Duty of Street Commissioner and Controller under Ordinance, - - - - - - - 141

Penalty for wilfully distroying, - - - 141

VACCINATION.

Compensation of Physician for - - - - 11

WARD COLLECTORS.

Bonds of - - - - - - - - 19

Powers and duties of - - - - - 19–20

Penalty for resisting, - - - - - - 20

WATCHMEN.

Uniform of - - - - - - - - 29

Bond of - - - - - - - - - 10

When on duty to wear Uniform, - - - - 8

Qualifications of - - - - - - 9

Duties of - - - - - 7–8–9–10–28

Time of duty of - - - - - - - 29

Under direction of Mayor and Marshal, - - - 28

WOOD.

Inspector of Firewood to measure, - - - - 24

www.ingramcontent.com/pod-product-compliance
Lightning Source LLC
LaVergne TN
LVHW021402110826
845150LV00007B/1756

* 9 7 8 1 4 2 5 5 1 2 7 0 5 *